Coke Studio (Season 14)

33 1/3 Global

33 1/3 Global, a series related to but independent from **33 1/3**, takes the format of the original series of short, music-based books and brings the focus to music throughout the world. With initial volumes focusing on Japanese and Brazilian music, the series will also include volumes on the popular music of Australia/Oceania, Europe, Africa, the Middle East, and more.

33 1/3 Japan

Series Editor: Noriko Manabe

Spanning a range of artists and genres—from the 1970s rock of Happy End to technopop band Yellow Magic Orchestra, the Shibuya-kei of Cornelius, classic anime series *Cowboy Bebop*, J-Pop/EDM hybrid Perfume, and vocaloid star Hatsune Miku—33 1/3 Japan is a series devoted to in-depth examination of Japanese popular music of the twentieth and twenty-first centuries.

Published Titles:
Supercell's *Supercell* by Keisuke Yamada
AKB48 by Patrick W. Galbraith and Jason G. Karlin
Yoko Kanno's *Cowboy Bebop Soundtrack* by Rose Bridges
Perfume's *Game* by Patrick St. Michel
Cornelius's *Fantasma* by Martin Roberts
Joe Hisaishi's *My Neighbor Totoro: Soundtrack* by Kunio Hara
Shonen Knife's *Happy Hour* by Brooke McCorkle
Nenes' *Koza Dabasa* by Henry Johnson
Yuming's *The 14th Moon* by Lasse Lehtonen
Kohaku utagassen: *The Red and White Song Contest* by Shelley Brunt
Toshiko Akiyoshi-Lew Tabackin Big Band's *Kogun* by E. Taylor Atkins
S.O.B.'s *Don't Be Swindle* by Mahon Murphy and Ran Zwigenberg

Forthcoming Titles:
Yellow Magic Orchestra's *Yellow Magic Orchestra* by Toshiyuki Ohwada

33 1/3 Brazil

Series Editor: Jason Stanyek

Covering the genres of samba, tropicália, rock, hip hop, forró, bossa nova, heavy metal and funk, among others, 33 1/3 Brazil is a series devoted to in-depth examination of the most important Brazilian albums of the twentieth and twenty-first centuries.

Published Titles:

Caetano Veloso's *A Foreign Sound* by Barbara Browning
Tim Maia's *Tim Maia Racional Vols. 1 & 2* by Allen Thayer
João Gilberto and Stan Getz's *Getz/Gilberto* by Brian McCann
Gilberto Gil's *Refazenda* by Marc A. Hertzman
Dona Ivone Lara's *Sorriso Negro* by Mila Burns
Milton Nascimento and Lô Borges's *The Corner Club* by Jonathon Grasse
Racionais MC's *Sobrevivendo no Inferno* by Derek Pardue
Naná Vasconcelos's *Saudades* by Daniel B. Sharp
Chico Buarque's *First Chico Buarque* by Charles A. Perrone

Forthcoming titles:

Jorge Ben Jor's *África Brasil* by Frederick J. Moehn

33 1/3 Europe

Series Editor: Fabian Holt

Spanning a range of artists and genres, 33 1/3 Europe offers engaging accounts of popular and culturally significant albums of Continental Europe and the North Atlantic from the twentieth and twenty-first centuries.

Published Titles:

Darkthrone's *A Blaze in the Northern Sky* by Ross Hagen
Ivo Papazov's *Balkanology* by Carol Silverman
Heiner Müller and Heiner Goebbels's *Wolokolamsker Chaussee* by Philip V. Bohlman

Modeselektor's *Happy Birthday!* by Sean Nye
Mercyful Fate's *Don't Break the Oath* by Henrik Marstal
Bea Playa's *I'll Be Your Plaything* by Anna Szemere and András Rónai
Various Artists' *DJs do Guetto* by Richard Elliott
Czesław Niemen's *Niemen Enigmatic* by Ewa Mazierska and Mariusz Gradowski
Massada's *Astaganaga* by Lutgard Mutsaers
Los Rodriguez's *Sin Documentos* by Fernán del Val and Héctor Fouce
Édith Piaf's *Récital 1961* by David Looseley
Nuovo Canzoniere Italiano's *Bella Ciao* by Jacopo Tomatis
Iannis Xenakis's *Persepolis* by Aram Yardumian
Vopli Vidopliassova's *Tantsi* by Maria Sonevytsky
Amália Rodrigues's *Amália at the Olympia* by Lila Ellen Gray
Ardit Gjebrea's *Projekt Jon* by Nicholas Tochka
Aqua's *Aquarium* by C.C. McKee
J.M.K.E.'s *To the Cold Land* by Brigitta Davidjants
Taco Hemingway's *Jarmark* by Kamila Rymajdo

Forthcoming Titles:
Tripes' *Kefali Gemato Hrisafi* by Dafni Tragaki
Silly's *Februar* by Michael Rauhut
CCCP's *Fedeli Alla Linea's 1964–1985 Affinità-Divergenze Fra Il Compagno Togliatti E Noi Del Conseguimento Della Maggiore Età* by Giacomo Bottà

33 1/3 Oceania

Series Editors: Jon Stratton (senior editor) and Jon Dale (specializing in books on albums from Aotearoa/New Zealand)

Spanning a range of artists and genres from Australian Indigenous artists to Maori and Pasifika artists, from Aotearoa/New Zealand noise music to Australian rock, and including music from Papua and other Pacific islands, 33 1/3 Oceania offers exciting accounts of albums that illustrate the wide range of music made in the Oceania region.

Published Titles:

John Farnham's *Whispering Jack* by Graeme Turner
The Church's *Starfish* by Chris Gibson
Regurgitator's *Unit* by Lachlan Goold and Lauren Istvandity
Kylie Minogue's *Kylie* by Adrian Renzo and Liz Giuffre
Alastair Riddell's *Space Waltz* by Ian Chapman
Hunters & Collectors's *Human Frailty* by Jon Stratton
The Front Lawn's *Songs from the Front Lawn* by Matthew Bannister
Bic Runga's *Drive* by Henry Johnson
The Dead C's *Clyma est mort* by Darren Jorgensen
Ed Kuepper's *Honey Steel's Gold* by John Encarnacao
Chain's *Toward the Blues* by Peter Beilharz
Hilltop Hoods' *The Calling* by Dianne Rodger
Screamfeeder's *Kitten Licks* by Ben Green and Ian Rogers
The Triffids' *Born Sandy Devotional* by Christina Ballico
John Sangster's *Lord of the Rings, Vols. 1–3* by Bruce Johnson
5MMM's *Compilation Album of Adelaide Bands 1980* by Collette Snowden
The Clean's *Boodle Boodle Boodle* by Geoff Stahl
The Avalanches' *Since I Left You* by Charles Fairchild
Soundtrack from *Saturday Night Fever* by Clinton Walker

Forthcoming Titles:

INXS' *Kick* by Ryan Daniel and Lauren Moxey
Sunnyboys' *Sunnyboys* by Stephen Bruel
Eyeliner's *BUY NOW* by Michael Brown
silverchair's *Frogstomp* by Jay Daniel Thompson
TISM's *Machiavelli and the Four Seasons* by Tyler Jenke
The La De Das' *The Happy Prince* by John Tebbutt
Crowded House's *Together Alone* by Barnaby Smith
Gary Shearston's *Dingo* by Peter Mills

Coke Studio (Season 14)

Rakae Rehman Jamil
and Khadija Muzaffar

33⅓ SOUTH ASIA

Series Editor: Natalie Sarrazin

BLOOMSBURY
NEW DELHI • LONDON • OXFORD • NEW YORK • SYDNEY

BLOOMSBURY INDIA
Bloomsbury Publishing India Pvt. Ltd
Second Floor, LSC Building No. 4, DDA Complex, Pocket C–6&7,
Vasant Kunj, New Delhi 110070

BLOOMSBURY, BLOOMSBURY ACADEMIC INDIA and the Diana logo are
trademarks of Bloomsbury Publishing Plc

First published in India 2025
First published in the United States of America 2025

This edition published with permission from Bloomsbury Publishing Plc,
50 Bedford Square, London, WC1B3DP, UK

A catalogue record for this book is available from the British Library.
A catalog record for this book is available from the Library of Congress.

ISBN: 978-93-61311-37-6

Typeset by Integra Software Services Pvt. Ltd.
Printed and bound in India by Replika Press Pvt. Ltd.

Contents

Acknowledgments xi

Introduction 1

Coke Studio Through the Years 5

Coke Studio: How Did Pakistani Music Get Here? 13

Coke Studio as an Insider: Rakae's Experiences as a Guest Artist and Audio Engineer 19

Season 14: Re-defining the Narrative 29

Sway in Ecstasy 33

Groovy Lament from Lyari 39

Ballad of the Superstars 43

A Soulful Melancholic Melody of Soothing Voices 47

A Punjabi Wedding Groove 51

An Anthem for the Marginalized 55

A Hard Rock and Rap Combo 59

A Melodic Banger with an Attitude 63

A Powerhouse Anthem from the Shafi Siblings 67

A Song about Being Carefree 71

A Funky Devotional Sonic Delight 73

Let's Go! 75

Until We Meet Again 77

Coke Studio's Great Comeback 79

Postmodern Vibe for a Postmodern Time 85

Bibliography 88
Index 92

Acknowledgments

This book would not have been possible to write without the aid and guidance of some people I would like to thank. First of all, I would like to thank Ali Hamza and Zohaib Kazi for helping me with acquiring permission from the Coca-cola Company to write this book. I would also like to thank them for entrusting me in my abilities as an audio engineer and an artist during season 11. Secondly, I would like to thank Prof. Natalie Sarrazin for giving me the opportunity to write this book and for her patience and encouragement. I would like to thank Zubair Mallick, who provided me with pictures of artists and the set from Season 14, and for connecting me with various artists for interviews which were crucial to this book. Furthermore, I wish to thank Noor Shiekh who provided me with a book she wrote titled "Beyond the Wave; Transcending Boundaries, Coke Studio Pakistan", which brilliantly summarizes each season of Coke Studio since its inception along with how the socio-political climate impacted music during this time. I would like to thank my interviewees, Jamal Rahman, Abdullah Siddiqui, Sherry Katthak and Faisal Kapadia for taking out the time for giving me crucial information for the book. Lastly, I wish to thank Khadija Muzaffar, the co-author of this book, for setting the tone of this book perfectly and adding her unique and holistic perspective on each song of season 14.

Introduction

Some things in life are just simply inescapable. You *will* spill your coffee on yourself on a day you're running late for work. You *will* miss the bus by a fraction of a millisecond, thereby being resigned to what seems like a lifetime of waiting at the bus stop. Just like that, if you are in Pakistan, chances are you *will* come across a Coke Studio song out in the wild. Maybe you're visiting a mall, or a grocery store, or are taking a cab or an Uber. Maybe you're at a wedding, a birthday, a work event. Whatever the occasion, Coke Studio seems to find its way into the playlist, the CD, the radio, and the sound system. And whatever song you hear will ultimately find its way into your brain, lodging itself there firmly, like a stubborn earworm.

That is both the magic and the curse of Coke Studio. A venture by the Coca-Cola Corporation that recognized a significant gap in Pakistan's music ecosystem, Coke Studio is a music TV show that has popular musicians come together and have a televised jam session. The musicians perform their own unique covers of iconic Pakistani folk and pop songs, and although the show started with a heavy emphasis on folk and Sufi rock, it has since ventured into other genres, as discussed later in the book. Coke Studio became an instant hit after its launch in 2008, and since then has been producing a new season each year without fail. To say that the music the show produces has become the most popular music in Pakistan overtime, would not be an understatement.

That being said, the show wasn't without its own share of criticism and controversy. As Coke Studio grew in popularity and began to dominate the music scene in Pakistan, several music critics and connoisseurs became skeptical of the company's intentions, subjecting the show to scrutiny and even disdain. Some artists argued that Coke Studio's dominance over the music industry in Pakistan was akin to them monopolizing the space and altering consumer preferences by only pushing music that was profitable for the Coca-Cola corporation. Others complained that the music was too derivative and unoriginal, or that it ruined a perfectly good song by turning it into an abominable cover. In an article written by Suleman Akhtar for *The Express Tribune*, he writes: "At the risk of sounding judgmental, let me state flat out that 'Coke Studio' is the place where a revitalization of folk culture is endeavored by slaughtering it … Meeting with the commercial needs of a rapidly expanding electronic media culture, folk culture was distastefully incorporated in the music vestiges and the outcome was a commercial success … The phenomenon, notwithstanding, cannot be accepted as some kind of a development by any standard of music and art. This is more of a distortion of 'original' than a revivification." (2012)

Others still took issue with the lack of representation of the diverse cultural landscape of Pakistan, despite Coke Studio's attempts at bringing folk culture to the mainstream. According to the 2022 edition of the Ethnologue, there are at least sixty-eight different languages spoken in Pakistan, out of which many, critics argued, go completely ignored in most seasons of Coke Studio. In an essay by Ayesha Le Breton, culture writer Ahmer Naqvi is quoted as saying, "There's a lot of seasons where the only language you hear is Punjabi, [with] just another sprinkling of some token inclusions." (2024)

Whatever the arguments against Coke Studio may have been, it cannot be denied that the show is a massive cultural juggernaut in the Pakistani media industry and has helped propel music in Pakistan, not just by reviving a dormant industry but also by helping create conversations and meaningful discourse about the role of music in Pakistani society.

Coke Studio Through the Years

The concept of Coke Studio was initially created in Brazil in 2007. According to Deepti Unni (2011) in her article on "The Challenge of Fusion," "Coke Studio began life in Brazil as *Estúdio Coca-Cola Zero*—a one-time marketing plan to sell pre-packaged music on Nokia 5310 phones—where two different Brazilian artists recorded a show fusing different styles of music." The concept of "fusion music" wasn't a completely revolutionary idea, but it had never really been formally explored in Pakistan, in a way that would bring it to the mainstream. Prior attempts at combining traditional and contemporary elements of Pakistani music were mostly based on the work and interests of musicians who worked independently and separately from one another. Coke Studio Pakistan changed that by bringing these musicians together on one platform. Launched in 2008, the studio featured collaborations between popular artists and classical/semi-classical and folk musicians in Pakistan. However, over time, the concept underwent a complete transformation in Pakistan, where it is known primarily as a platform for visually showcasing musical collaborations between Pakistani contemporary and traditional musicians. Although Coke Studio is presented to listeners as a reality television show, it is also an initiative that brings together Pakistan's most innovative music producers, who are really the ones behind the overall soundscape and ideas presented in the music.

As a televised show, Coke Studio has received critical acclaim, often described as a revolutionary step in bridging the cultural barriers existing in Pakistan. In a recent article on Coke Studio, Bilal Tanweer (2012) writes, "Coke Studio emerged, as a clear attempt to bridge the cultural fragmentation of Pakistan … through Coke Studio, many folk musicians and their work has been introduced to a new generation and allowed them to access a deep and rich cultural heritage that was withering on the margins." As thus, the show has helped revive many forgotten folk traditions and cultural relics that would likely not have been otherwise accessed by the common public.

Coke Studio offers a platform, equipped with the latest tools in digital recording and production, for musicians all around Pakistan to create music. The show has offered unique interpretations of pop and folk songs that combined digitized sounds and effects applied to acoustic percussive and melodic instruments. This book explores what it is that makes Coke Studio unique from other recording studios and how these musical interpretations are executed, through a thorough review of Season 14 of the show as well as the unique experiences of the authors; Rakae's as an audio engineer and an artist within prior seasons of the show, and Khadija's as a music journalist and academic. In this book we explain how the show's main producers set out to create an entirely unique tone for each season through a combination of genre-bending musical innovations, soundscapes, and production techniques, while holding on to the central idea of celebrating the elusive multi-headed giant that is Pakistani identity.

We chose to highlight Season 14 in particular as it took several risks which other seasons did not, such as featuring a diverse array of artists, and not just Uber popular big names. It was, at the time of writing of this book, the latest season of the show. Season 14 showcased artists who were known for singing songs that were deemed suitable only for Pakistan's film industry called Lollywood, often containing vulgar lyrical content and generic grooves that did not require high levels of musicianship. They took those artists and turned them into innovators, using their strengths and skills to represent a vibe and a hybrid form of music which pertained to the sensibilities of Pakistan's emerging youth. Similarly, to appeal to the tastes of said youth, Season 14 also featured many new, rising musicians, who could be described as indie artists that fall into the unique phenomenon of bedroom pop. These self-made musicians were all young and majorly popular amongst the youth of the country, so it only made sense for Coke Studio to include them in the folds of its platform.

After a successful fifteen-year run, and a very successful fourteenth season, Coke Studio is now on Season 15, which launched on April 15, 2024, and is modeled very much after its precursor, signaling to the impact of Season 14 on its aesthetic and aural decisions. Each prior season of Coke Studio showcased a unique set of artists and highlighted certain themes and elements pertaining to Pakistani culture and society. And over time, as the show changed hands, the unique approaches of each of its showrunners become apparent. Season 1 introduced the central idea of fusion music, by presenting mainstream Pakistani music fused with Western elements, through songs like sufi-rock band Junoon's "Garaj Baras" performed as a duet between Junoon lead vocalist Ali Azmat and qawwali superstar Rahat Fateh Ali Khan. Season 2 established Coke Studio as a powerful tool for bringing Pakistani folk and popular musicians together, thereby bridging the rural and the urban, as well as transcending the boundaries of viewership across the world through digital platforms such as YouTube. Popular songs from the season, such as Zeb and Haniya's "Paimona," have amassed over 2.4 million views on the video viewing platform.

Season 3 solidified the powerful impact of folk tunes blended with solid funky grooves, such as pop powerhouse Meesha Shafi's and folk music extraordinaire Arif Lohar's mega-hit "Alif Allah." The popularity of Season 4 ignited India's desire to launch their own version of Coke Studio in 2011, whilst season 5's "Kangna"—a sufi qawwali track sung by Fareed Ayaz and Abu Mian qawwal—was picked up for Hollywood's cinematic adaptation of Pakistani author Mohsin Hamid's *The Reluctant Fundamentalist*. This was also when Coke Studio's Middle Eastern chapter was initiated. Season 6 went beyond the borders of Pakistan and brought in musicians from Bangladesh, Nepal, Turkey, Italy, Serbia, Morocco, and Norway, and around this time, Coke Studio Africa was launched.

Seasons 7–10 brought about a major change in the production side; producer Rohail Hyatt was replaced with Bilal Maqsood and Faisal Kapadia, who were the duo behind the acclaimed Pakistani band Strings, which was responsible for producing timeless hits such as "Sar Kiye Ye Paahar" and "Duur." The Strings era of Coke Studio brought about a steady number of hits such as pop superstar Atif Aslam's rendition of "Tajdar-e-Haram," newcomer Momina Mustehsan and qawwali megastar Rahat Fateh Ali Khan's take on his legendary uncle Nusrat Fateh Ali Khan's famous hit "Afreen Afreen." During this time, the concept of bringing in multiple producers to handle three to four songs each, as opposed to having one producer run the whole show was also introduced. Although Coke Studio focused less on experimentation in terms of soundscapes and themes under Maqsood and Kapadia, they in their own way came up with effective and unique collaborations between artists that garnered timeless pieces of music that are well loved to this day.

In 2018, Coke Studio again changed direction and decided to replace Strings as the main producers of the show and work with musicians Zohaib Kazi and Ali Hamza instead for Season 11. Zohaib Kazi had prior experience with Coke Studio in production and management for the first seven seasons and had also produced several audio/visual albums of his own, whilst Ali Hamza—one of the lead members of the popular Pakistani rock band Noori—had launched himself as a solo artist during the previous year and had been a guest music producer for three songs on Season 10 of the show. Season 11 was one of Coke Studio's most ambitious ones yet. It included two modules of the show, one of which was titled "Coke Studio Explorer," which showcased a total of five songs from five different regions of Pakistan. To this end, Ali Hamza and Zohaib traveled to Sindh, Balochistan, Punjab, Chitral, and Azad Kashmir, all the while documenting and recording the music of the artists featured there, as well as shooting music videos in those regions. Coke Studio Explorer received mostly favorable reviews in the media for its focus on diversity, inclusion of the ethnic minorities of Pakistan and its unique approach to the videos in a style that had never been done before.

The second module acted as the main season and featured thirty-one songs. It included a promotional song titled "Hum Dekhengay" (We shall see), which was an adaptation of a famous poem written by the revolutionary Pakistani poet Faiz Ahmad Faiz, who was known for his scathing political commentary, which often left him at odds with the then-military dictator's regime. The choice to include this song, not only as the season promo but also a mere three days before the 2018 general election which so many were expecting to fall victim to military intervention yet again, raised a variety of concerns and doubts over the season's success due to its political connotations. As a result, the producers had no choice but to omit certain lyrics from this version so as to not offend certain political figures of the Pakistani government. Nonetheless, the track, which included all the artists singing one verse each from the celebrated poem, was received positively. Following the promo song, the rest of the songs were released as episodes each week, with each episode containing around three to four songs. Every episode represented a certain theme, and the songs were then chosen according to that theme. For example, Season 11's fifth episode was titled *"Mauj"* which is the Urdu word for entertainment, and one of the songs on that episode—Aima Baig and Sahir Ali Bagga's rendition of Saraiki folk classic "Malang"—was described by the show's YouTube channel as an "interesting festive mix" due to its "diverse musical elements and zesty groove" that "casts the net even wider with the melodious Bansuri and it's sporadic Banjo beats." With each song, a BTS or "Behind The Scenes" video would be released during the morning whilst the full song with the video was released in the evening. This was standard for every Coke Studio season. In addition, the visual element of the videos was vibrant and at times could feel a little overwhelming due to the constant flashing of lights in some of them.

The next couple of seasons were produced by Coke Studio's first producer Rohail Hyatt, as the show's executives aimed at trying to bring back the show's original soundscape back into the foreground in order to garner more listenership and popularity. Unlike Season 11, which had a more experimental, gritty, and at times rebellious tone in the songs used, Season 12 focused more on soulful, melodic, and regional tunes.

Season 12 began with the soulful rendition of the late Nusrat Fateh Ali Khan's timeless *hamd* "Wohi Khuda Hai," sung by Atif Aslam. The song received somewhat favorable reviews but did not garner as much appreciation as his previous hit "Tajdar-e-Haram," perhaps because the rendition focused more on maintaining its soulful and contemplative vibe sonically rather than creating a dynamic ebb and flow of musical parts and vocal melodies that the former employed. In addition, the visual aspect of the show went back to its original style, with calm and steady shots and less changes and camera angles, and slower in pace as compared to the previous season.

Coke Studio's thirteenth season faced its biggest challenge yet, having to navigate its way through the aftermath of the COVID-19 Pandemic, as the show faced massive delays in production due to the worldwide catastrophe. Hyatt and the Coke executives had to adjust accordingly due to the pandemic, and this meant that artists had to be recorded individually in the studio space, requiring extreme social distancing and creating social bubbles in order to limit the risk of spreading the virus. This also resulted in a smaller amount of audio tracks; around twelve, which was the lowest number of songs to be featured in a season. Nonetheless, the show still made quite an impact, opening with all-female anthem "Na Tutteya Ve" rendered by vocalists Meesha Shafi, Sanam Marvi, Fariha Pervaiz, Zara Madni, Wajiha Naqvi, and Sehar Gul Khan. The song conveys equality from a woman's perspective, and speaks about "the toll of microaggressions that women, especially working women, have to face every day and how there is strength and vulnerability" (Dawn, 2020). In addition, due to the pandemic, Hyatt decided only to use urban artists, since it was easier for him to send his mobile recording unit in order for them to record their parts individually, and they had been given instructions to learn how to use this unit themselves. More importantly, this was the first time that a season focused purely on original compositions, which all twelve of the songs were. This was a step that inspired Coke Studio's penultimate fourteenth season to follow and execute as well.

Coke Studio: How Did Pakistani Music Get Here?

The implementation of digital recording and production practices in Pakistan stems from the trend of incorporating Western styles of music such as jazz, rock, hip-hop, and disco, with Urdu lyrics. This trend especially dominated the Pakistani music scene during the 1980s, a time when electronic instruments such as the keyboard and electric guitar were regularly used in Western popular music genres. However, the appreciation of these genres of music began to take root in the late 1960s with the growing utilization of Western musical styles in film music. According to journalist and culture critic Nadeem Farooq Paracha (2004), during this era, Ahmed Rushdie, a vocalist of film music, incorporated a blend of bubble-gum pop, rock-and-roll twist music, and Pakistani film music, which eventually came to be known as "filmi-pop" music.

In the early 1970s, modern Pakistani music was taken out of the confines of the genre of "filmi-pop" music and was instead practiced as an independent form of popular music. The first artist to begin this trend was Alamgir, who was considered the "Elvis of the East" (Abbas, Dawn). He sang his first hit single "Albela Rahi" for one of the country's first musical program series, *Sunday ke Sunday* launched by Karachi Television between 1973 and 1974. During the early 1980s, Alamgir experimented further by blending Punjabi folk tunes with Western popular music, such as the song "Jugni" (Paracha, 2018). Around the same time, the sibling duo of Nazia and Zohaib Hassan also gained success, cementing their place as pop icons with their style of electronic disco music fused with traditional Pakistani tunes, resulting in hit songs like "Disco Deewanay" and "Aap Jesa Koi." Much of their music was recorded in music studios of the state-owned Pakistan Television (PTV), which were located in the metropolitan cities of Karachi and Lahore. The trend of fusing Western styles with Pakistani musical idioms continued to grow as listeners showed greater appreciation for Nazia and Zohaib's timeless songs.

As a result of the rising influence of popular Western musical traditions on Pakistani music, the main centers for music recording in Pakistan, such as the PTV, shifted their focus from art musical styles to the popular forms of music. Recording and producing works of the traditional styles of music at these state-owned studios began to decline. One of the main reasons for this decline was because the popular forms of music generated more financial income for the recording companies. With the increasing demand by the general Pakistani audience for these emerging musical styles, multinational corporations began to invest in recording studios primarily for the sake of using these styles for their advertising campaigns. As a result, many folk and classical artists such as Pathanay Khan, Reshma, and Ustad Sharif Khan of Poonchwalay sought privately owned recording studios to record their music, which were relatively few during the 1980s. One example of such a studio was located at the Sanjan Nagar Institute of Philosophy of Arts (SIPA), which catered solely to recording traditional Pakistani music.

Shortly after Nazia and Zohaib's reign over the popular music scene in Pakistan, came another fusion musical act. The band Vital Signs, formed in 1986, became the first group to fuse

Western rock musical elements with the region's traditional melodies and Urdu lyrics. The band was created by two musicians from Rawalpindi: a bass guitarist named Shahzad Hassan, and a keyboard player by the name of Rohail Hyatt, who later on went to become the first and current producer of Coke Studio. The band then added another member, lead vocalist Junaid Jamshed. The music of Vital Signs was heavily influenced by Western rock bands such as Pink Floyd, Rush, and A-ha, and even performed covers of their songs in various concerts at college functions, private parties, and dinner events. Their first breakthrough appeared with their debut album *Vital Signs 1*, which was recorded at Electronic and Music Industries (EMI) studios in Karachi in 1987. This album offered a fresh new style of music which appealed to the younger generation of the country. It also led to the emergence of many other bands who tried to replicate this new style of pop/rock music. In addition, they were also cost-effective as they contained a plethora of digitally synthesized instrumental sounds. Thus, almost all bands or artists in Pakistan at the time used keyboard synthesizers in their music.

During the early 1990s, the sufi-rock band Junoon took the place of Vital Signs as one of the most recognized and acclaimed bands of all time in Pakistan. Junoon became widely appreciated by a variety of audiences in Pakistan because their style of music blended Western rock music with poetry of famous Pakistani poets such as Bulleh Shah and Allama Iqbal. In addition, they also addressed political issues and concerns, which led many people in Pakistan to relate to their music even more.

Similarly, the late Nusrat Fateh Ali Khan, one of Pakistan's most renowned qawwali singers, experimented with Western musical styles by collaborating with Michael Brook. In an article written by Paul Tingen for the 1995 edition of the music magazine *Sound on Sound*, both artists worked together to produce an album called "Night Songs," which was made "in a decidedly hi-tech manner, with sampling, digital editing, looping, sonic manipulation and all" (par. 2). The album was widely appreciated amongst audiences not only in Pakistan, but across the world. It also signified how Nusrat Fateh Ali Khan, along with other qawwali musicians, received worldwide acclaim due to their experimental recordings and performances in Western countries. According to Regula Qureshi from her article titled "His Master's Voice? Exploring *Qawwali* and 'Gramophone Culture' in South Asia" (1999), "It was their entry into the Western World Music circuit with concerts reinforced by recordings that gradually invested Ghulam Farid Sabri and especially Nusrat Fateh Ali Khan with stardom" (29). These qawwals were already huge stars in their own countries, but the exposure to Western audiences—both diaspora and not—had helped their fame skyrocket even more.

As digital recording technologies continued to develop, the prices for recording and production equipment began to diminish considerably. This made it possible for musicians to purchase the necessary equipment that was imported from other countries (usually from the UK or the United States) and set up recording studios in their own private spaces, such as in a single room located in their own homes. All one needed was a computer, a digital DAW, recording gear such as microphones, and a device called an Audio Interface, which was used as the bridge between recording gear and the computer. This created a generation of musicians who also played the role of music producer in Pakistan, thereby inadvertently contributing to "bedroom pop" long before the term was even coined. Pop and rock artists such as Noori, Entity/Paradigm (EP), and

Mekaal Hassan, who were all based in Lahore, began recording and producing their music by setting up their own personal recording studios at home. Mekaal Hassan, a musician well-versed in Western music theory and a guitarist known for playing improvisational jazz, began to experiment with his music with the use of digital technologies. He created an analog/digital recording studio for fusing classical *khayal bandishes*, or compositions based on the Ragas of North Indian music, and Pakistani folk songs with his repertoire of jazz harmonies and rhythms. His recording studio is now known as "Digital Fidelity Studios," where he produces not only his own compositions but also recordings of other Pakistani popular and folk artists. In 2022, when his studio completely burned down due to an electronic malfunction, many musicians and artists all over the country launched a campaign to help donate toward the reconstruction of the studio.

During the last twenty years, music producers and artists, popular, traditional, and underground musicians and bands, continue to expand their musical boundaries through the use of digital audio equipment. Artists such as Sajid and Zeeshan made songs that incorporated digital sounds and effects with the acoustic guitar and the human voice. Shiraz Uppal, a student of A. R. Rahman, India's most renowned Bollywood music producer, created his own style of Urdu pop music by combining traditionally influenced melodies with digitally produced percussive samples and stringed sounds, such as the violin, synthesized pads, and even the mandolin. Kaavish, a band based in Karachi, became known for creating a musical style that blends Western harmonies and orchestral instruments with folk and semi-classical based melodies of Pakistani music. In a conversation with the lead vocalist of the band, Jaffer Zaidi, Rakae asked him whether digital recording and production practices have had a positive impact on the music of Pakistan. Jaffer responded, "It obviously has had a positive impact, we haven't made the most of it is a different thing altogether, although Coke Studio can be regarded as a step in the right direction."

Coke Studio as an Insider: Rakae's Experiences as a Guest Artist and Audio Engineer

In addition to being a musician and musicologist, Rakae's unique insight into Coke Studio also comes from the fact that he has worked and been involved in two prior seasons of the show. In Season 2, Rakae was a guest artist and played sitar on three of the songs that season, while in Season 11 his role expanded to the pre-production aspect of Coke Studio. Below, he shares his experiences from both seasons, and explores the difference in style between both:

> I was fortunate to have participated in seasons 2 and 11 of Coke Studio. In season 2 I had been featured as a guest artist, specifically as a sitar player, on three of the songs performed by renowned pop/rock band Noori. During this time, Rohail Hyatt was the main producer of the show, who has since then produced over eight seasons of Coke Studio, from seasons one to six, and then 12 and 13 respectively.
>
> In Season 11, I had somewhat of a larger role, and was involved in the second half of the pre-production phase where I was tasked with editing the songs for Coke Studio

Explorer, as well as being a stage manager and an audio engineer. I was also brought on during the production, and primarily the post-production phase as a guest artist, due to being one of the members of the instrumental funk band Mughal-e-Funk, which was one of the featured artists of the main module of the show. I describe both experiences as feeling surreal; to be able to meet some of the top musicians of the country and to play with them on the same platform, and to be a part of Pakistan's biggest music show was all a bit overwhelming, but I had relished both opportunities. However, my main reason for sharing my experiences lies in the process involved in the production of the music, and how it compares to the way it was done in season 14.

In season 2, which took place in 2009, the music making process at Coke Studio took place in two phases. The first phase entailed the non-recorded exchange between the main artist, folk musicians and the house band. The house band at Coke Studio consisted of some of the most experienced musicians of the Pakistani music industry who were required to play in all the thirty songs that were recorded for every season. These musicians were highly skilled in playing both Western and local instruments and had ample experience playing for the Pakistani music industry. The house band had been a regular feature since the studio's launch.

Before going to Coke Studio, I was approached by Ali Noor during the month of November to come over to his house and improvise with the sitar on one of his own compositions that was going to be featured at the studio, which he sent, and Hyatt approved. I remember feeling overjoyed upon realizing that I was going to get a chance to play at the studio. The first step is for the main artists to send a sample recording of their songs digitally to Rohail Hyatt in the form of an mp3. Hyatt then gives his own analysis and feedback on the mix, in terms of its structure, layout and how the classical or traditional instrumentalist/vocalist can add their input to the song.

In the next phase, I was asked to travel to Karachi along with Ali Noor and Ali Hamza and spent time with the house band at the studio to practice the three songs of their segment that was going to be recorded for the live television show. The time was scheduled during February so as to give the musicians a month to figure out the respective parts they would play in the songs. During this time, we spent three to four days playing with the house band at the studio, thus also utilizing the space for rehearsals and musical experimentation. This allowed for a flow of musical exchange and familiarity to be created between the artists. Once our musical ideas were synthesized, the rehearsals of the songs were re-recorded by Hyatt in the studio's recording room.

Around the end of March, Hyatt would record the final versions of the songs that would be produced and released nation-wide during the end of May, since that would give him enough time to work on the post-production of the recordings. In March, during the final recordings, we were given another three days to practice, so as to obtain the correct flow for the fourth and final day, during which Hyatt recorded the performance. On the final day, we all sat in our respective positions, each person having a pair of in-ear monitors so as to clearly hear their own instruments. Since the ensemble consisted of a drummer, two main vocalists, three backing vocalists, a violinist, a lead guitarist, a *dholak player*, a bassist, and myself on the sitar, it would have been difficult for the musicians to hear themselves without the in-ear monitors.

After performing a practice run through, Hyatt would inform us that he would start recording the next run-through. During all of this, there would be video cameramen floating about the room taking photos and recording everyone while they were in action. I recall there was a glass panel placed in front of me on the circular platform I was sitting on, so as to block any extraneous sound coming into the microphone placed in front of me. Furthermore, there was also a small screen placed in front of me that displayed the tempo of the song being played, as well as cues that alerted me that my part in the song was about to come. In any case, Hyatt made sure that the songs were recorded several times (usually two or three attempts) to account for any musical errors or shortcomings that may have occurred during each take.

After playing the songs three times each, everyone in the studio, which included the crew members and other artists who were going to perform next after the current segment, gave the current artists a round of applause and congratulated them on a job well done. However, it would not be until the end of May that any of us would hear the final versions of the recordings, since Hyatt needed that amount of time to refine and create mastered mixes of the songs during the post-production phase, which is always a time consuming and demanding process. Thus, the post-production process gave both the artist and producer a chance to add their own musical input to the final versions of the music.

Nine years later, when shooting for Coke Studio Season 11, I found the process to be quite similar in terms of putting the songs together, but this time I became a part of the core team of the season. I remember being approached by Ali Hamza and Zohaib Kazi to help out with the post-production of Coke Studio Explorer, which aimed to highlight the depth of Pakistani identity. Ali Hamza said, "We wanted to focus on things that we hadn't ever explored before, and to look at elements of what makes Pakistan what it is today, highlighting the Pakistani identity and truly owning the white in our flag." Through this initiative, they wanted to shift the focus from the urban demographic to the rural one. Hamza and Kazi traveled to five different regions of Pakistan, recorded, and shot music videos with five different groups of musicians. Once they had all the material and audio recorded, which was around February of 2018, I was brought on board to help with the editing and post-production phase of the five songs.

The music was primarily a combination of organic instrumentation, such as the dholak from Punjab, the *dambur* from Sindh, along with the regional voices, with electronic musical elements and phrases added by Zohaib Kazi, and resulting in a completely unique interpretation of Pakistani folk songs that most had not come across before. I remember losing all concept of time while working on editing the tracks, as I was so immersed in the new sound that Zohaib had created for the recordings. I can only describe it as a unique blend between electronically synthesized sonic elements with local percussive and melodic instruments specific to each region they traveled to, and I remember being driven by discovering the shape the songs would take at the end. Once the tracks were complete and ready to mix,

I sat with Zohaib while he worked on the mixes, after which they would watch them overlayed on top of the videos, which still feels surreal to me.

If you thought that after completing a lengthy project like CS Explorer, the producers and showrunners would have wanted some time off, you would be highly mistaken, especially when it came to Coke Studio. Once the production for CS Explorer concluded, it was time for work on the seasons' main show to begin. I was given the task of working as an audio technician for the pre-production phase, which meant helping set up the audio equipment at the location where the video and audio recordings for the songs would take place. Since showrunners Kazi and Hamza intended to finalize thirty-four songs in just two weeks, I and the audio team had only two days to get the task of setting up the audio equipment. This involved hooking up all the required hardware, such as the audio interfaces, the microphones, pre-amps, the desktop, and the mixers together with the necessary cables. The audio team also had to make sure that around sixty-four cables were labeled correctly, as a total of sixty-four instruments could possibly be recorded simultaneously just for one song. Such was the magic and ambition of Coke Studio.

Once the setup was complete, the video and audio production process began swiftly. The day would usually begin around 11:00 am and the shoots would continue up to the wee hours of the morning, sometimes even ending around 5:00 am. The equipment would first be turned on to make sure everything was in working order. Then, according to the song and the artist that was being recorded that day, I and the audio team would plug in all the necessary cables and place the instruments accordingly. Once the setup was complete, each member of the audio engineering team, along with the house band, would check to see if the microphone signals were functioning properly. In addition, each musician had a personal monitoring device which they could connect headphones to in order to adjust the volume of other musical instruments according to their own personal auditory needs. Then the main artists would show up around an hour before the recording was slated to begin, during which I had to prep each artist for their song, making sure they were familiar with the cues and the arrangement of the song in question. Usually this would not take too much time and effort as most of the artists were already prepared and had some prior experience with recording studios. However, for the ones who were experiencing recording sessions for the first time in such a huge setup, I recall it being challenging to help them navigate their way in the recording process.

An example that sticks out is when during Ustaad Riaz Qadri's recording session with pop duo Krewella, it took them all a while to get used to singing with the metronome playing in their headphones. I, the producers and other members of the house band had to spend at least two hours guiding them and making them comfortable with singing to a metronome. Once this was taken care of, the actual recording took place, for which all the members of the house band, the guest artists, and the producers and engineers in the control room would take their positions. Once this was all figured out, the recording process would begin. It usually took three attempts to account for any errors that may occur, and to be able to give the post-production team several options to work with, so they could pick and choose the most optimal visual and sonic takes. Once this was taken care of, the artists would all take their spots on the set, and I and the audio engineering team would make sure everyone was placed in their proper positions with their microphones and cue machines functioning. Then I and the rest of the audio engineering crew would promptly scuttle back into the control room where all the audio and visual screens were located, and the producers would give the go ahead to begin both audio and video recordings. This process was applied in all songs throughout the season, of course with a few minor glitches, perhaps a microphone malfunctioning, or the desktop system freezing during one of the recordings, or perhaps one of the video camera's memory cards were full and had to be replaced during the middle of the shoot! Nonetheless, all thirty-four songs were recorded in a span of two and a half weeks, which was quite a task to be done in such a short span of time.

Once the production phase of the season was complete, the post-production phase began after a break of one week. The post-production phase lasted a total of around four months, and required the audio engineering team to work intensely on editing, cleaning and choosing the best takes for each song. This required us to work long hours, and sometimes even spend nights at the office that was rented out for the pre-production and post-production work. I remember I would sometimes have to sit six hours at a stretch editing a song, tuning the vocals and cleaning the audio for each track. Although it was time-consuming, frustrating and at times felt incredibly monotonous, the end result and the release dates kept me hugely motivated to complete and deliver the work.

Once we edited all thirty-four audio tracks, Mekaal Hasan, one of Pakistan's most experienced music producers who was known for producing the albums of Pop/rock band Noori and Atif Aslam, Pakistan's biggest pop sensation, joined in as the mixing engineer for the season. In a duration of a month, he was given the mammoth task of mixing all songs in such a short span of time, and needed all the help and extra ears he could get from the audio engineering team. I was fortunate to have sat and learned the mixing process from him, and he did a tremendous job with the mixes considering there were some minor flaws in the recording and production process of the audio during the production phase, such as extreme leakage of the drums into the other microphones used to record the vocals and other instruments in the setup, a common oversight that sometimes affected the mixes in previous seasons. Nevertheless, all these minor hurdles were soon forgotten once the songs were released, which was October 20, 2018.

Season 14: Re-defining the Narrative

Coke Studio's fourteenth season, which aired on January 14, 2022, came at a time when people across the world were gradually returning to normal functionality due to the 2020 COVID-19 pandemic, and there was finally a sense of hope and positivity at the beginning of the year. In the two years that the pandemic lasted, musical content in Pakistan had exponentially surged due to musicians and artists having the ability to stay home and churn out content on Instagram, or post YouTube videos of their individual performances. This had been a period where people had no choice but to stay home, and therefore, even aspiring musicians with regular day jobs now had the time to experiment creatively and put out a lot of music.

Despite all of this musical progress within the last two years, the act of getting a whole group of people together to create a show was nothing short of a tall task. However, the show's directors, producers, and managers were adamant to keep the momentum of the series going. Operating, planning, and executing a whole music production had its challenges, and things had to be done virtually in its initial phase. Even without the threat of a pandemic hanging over their heads, the prior season, Season 13, had taken over two years to be released, and it had only consisted of twelve songs spread across four episodes. This was almost half the number of songs compared to the previous seasons, and yet it had still taken longer. Speaking to Rakae about the initial stages of Coke Studio 14, Abdullah Siddiqui, who is a 24-year-old electronic music producer from Lahore, and was also one of the executive producers of Season 14, said, "We began [the creative process] in March of 2021, and at that point COVID was still kind of at its peak, so we were doing a lot of Zoom meetings to try and come up with a line-up."

Featuring thirteen songs, Season 14's main strength was in innovation and experimentation. This was the first season of the show produced by Zulfiqar Jabbar Khan, more popularly known as Xulfi, since Rohail Hyatt had once again stepped down from the role of showrunner. Xulfi was not afraid to take risks and change the game both sonically and visually, and thus, he took an entirely different approach in both perspectives. Xulfi has had a long career in music, and has greatly contributed to the music industry in Pakistan, both through the various bands he has been part of or founded, as well as the music shows he has helped spearhead. He is the founding member of critically acclaimed Pakistani rock bands Entity Paradigm (EP) and Call, has produced multiple successful albums for other bands such as Jal and Roxen, and has been the music producer of Coke Studio's competitor Nescafe Basement since 2012. The premise of Nescafe Basement is similar to Coke Studio in that they both focus on covers of pre-existing songs, but the difference lies in the fact that while Coke Studio features already established musicians and artists, Nescafe Basement features young, talented but unknown college students all handpicked and mentored by Xulfi himself, once again pointing to his open-minded approach to creativity. While the show received praise for the quality and variety of music, as well as the creative direction by Xulfi himself, it never reached the level of success Coke Studio enjoys.

In terms of the music for Coke Studio Season 14, Xulfi decided to utilize the skills of young producers who were proficient in electronic music production. Producers Talal Qureshi, Zain Ali—who is known professionally as Action Zain—and Abdullah Siddiqui, had all made a significant impact on the younger demographic with their music over the last decade as a whole, particularly during the last few years. Xulfi knew that Coke Studio needed a change in direction, and involving the newer generation was the way to implement it. A multitude of different vibes were introduced in Coke Studio, and the resultant sound seemed to transcend all barriers of culture, age, and genre, thereby generating a universal appeal rather than one specific to a certain region, country, or soundscape.

About the culturally ambiguous feel of the season, Siddiqui explained to Rakae, "What I love about electronic music is that it's not inherently tied to any culture, like when you are going back to the source of oscillators and sound waves, then you're just manipulating sound at a very primal level. There are certain vocabularies for how that's approached in different cultures, like electronic music from Europe or from the United States, they have different analogies, but conceptually it has no cultural ties."

Traditionally, the setup for Coke Studio used to be a studio-like environment, with the musicians and the house band spread across a giant room, while the featured artists would be in the center. Visually, everything would be in the signature Coca-Cola red and black, and glowing neon signs would cast a warm scarlet hue on everyone in the dimly lit room. The idea was for the audience to feel like they were simply watching a televised jam session between all the big names in music; it was supposed to feel casual and almost chaotic in its energy. Season 14, however, defied the norm of Coke Studio set design and introduced a new aesthetic where each of the thirteen songs had a specially curated and crafted set design, in accordance with their unique mood and theme. Each visual set was designed after taking into consideration the artists and the content of the song; and the clothes worn by the artists, the props, and the lighting were tailored to that specific visual setting. Even a casual viewing of any of the releases makes the distinct narrative behind each song, artist, and visuals very apparent. Jamal Rehman, who was a former music producer and owner of True Brew Records—a recording studio and gig space based in Lahore until its closure a couple of years ago—and has now moved on to doing film scores was the video director for Season 14's song "Kana Yaari." He mentioned to Rakae how he was asked by Xulfi to recognize who these artists are and where they come from, and amplify those aspects and the emotions they are portraying in the song through its visual depiction. Jamal said that he had to find a middle ground between music video and live performance and took inspiration from theater to achieve this task.

This is precisely what makes this season stand out as compared to other seasons: the fact that Coke Studio is no longer a solely auditory experience, but rather has expanded into a more meaningful audio-visual project with a life of its own. Granted, prior seasons had accompanying music videos as well. However, where older Coke Studio music videos were just a bonus accompaniment, the videos for Season 14 are essential to the narrative of the song. You can learn more about the narrative, the theme, and mood of each song by its music video, which wasn't necessarily true in the past. This careful balance between sound and visual was created meticulously by the producers of Season 14, and the results speak for themselves.

Sway in Ecstasy

The first track of Coke Studio Season 14 was scheduled to release on Friday, January 14, 2022. Millions of Pakistanis were waiting in anticipation for this release, as two legendary stalwarts of Pakistani music; Abida Parveen, a legendary semi-classical and Sufi *kalaam* vocalist, and Naseebo Lal, a popular folk and film song vocalist, were announced as the main vocalists to be featured on this track. Rakae had been ecstatic and impatient to hear it for two reasons, the first being that the song was being produced by Xulfi, who had previously produced five seasons of Nescafe Basement which had given Coke Studio's previous seasons stiff competition in terms of the quality of music. The second reason was due to Abdullah Siddiqui being credited as one of the music producers of the track, which meant that the audience was in for a treat.

The song and the video received positive reviews across the nation. In one article it was described as "hypnotically nostalgic as it is new" (*Daily Times*, 2022). The two legends sang an original titled "Tu Jhoom," and one cannot help but feel elated and inspired after listening to it. Conceptually, "Tu Jhoom" fits the classic spiritual and devotional Sufi narrative, literally meaning "Sway in Ecstasy." The song is about the soul's desire to find happiness and satisfaction from within themselves regardless of what has been achieved and discovered in the external world. Sonically, the track fuses synthesized percussive sounds and ambient and melodic elements with acoustic traditional instruments such as the tabla, played by Asif Ali, acoustic guitar played by Rohail Nawab, and the mountain dulcimer played by Awais Ali Kazmi.

This is nothing new for Coke Studio; they have always featured such experimental endeavors with the music, but what strikes the audience is the simplicity of the idea; to pair these two together and create a track that, as Abdullah Siddiqui states, is "quintessentially desi, but in a post-modern way." Furthermore, even though these two have been singing for decades, this is the first time they have been paired together for a collaboration. This is because of how the music they practice is generally perceived in society. Siddiqui points out how "putting these two women together is a huge statement," because you have "one woman who has been deified as a spiritual voice for many generations, and another woman who comes from a tradition of media that has always been otherized and cast aside as low-brow or not sophisticated enough … and the statement there is that that distinction is not valid, and that these women can be allowed to take the same space and take the same stage and send out the same message." Thus, with its first release, Season 14 addresses and challenges cultural stigmas that often act as destructive barriers for creating meaningful pieces of music in Pakistan.

The song opens up with a synthetic pad playing the tonic note in a slightly pumping-like movement known as the "sidechain" effect, followed by a short melody on the flute, eventually leading to the opening lines of the verse sung by Naseebo Lal with a soft bass drum hit. The treatment of the vocals is clear, evocative, and powerful, whilst the supporting music blends fluidly with her voice, while the melody has a sensibility resembling that of a Pakistani folk tune. Once her part ends with a few repetitions of the main refrain "Tu Jhoom," Abida Parveen begins her part, and the main rhythmic groove begins along with it. This is followed by the main line, "Tu Jhoom," being repeated by Parveen supported by a group of backing vocalists. The tone is set, and you are immediately immersed in the soundscape and the voices of the two stalwarts. The tabla groove blends so effortlessly with the electronic beat laid down by Siddiqui, and it creates a new soundscape that gives a sound similar to how Indian music producer A. R. Rahman's film songs in the 1990s were designed.

Once Parveen's part concludes, there is a drop in the music and the beat halts for a while. Lal enters with the second verse of the song with the lines "Mein raazi apni zaat tu / Mein utti apni auqat toon," which translates to "I am satisfied and content with my being, God has blessed me more than which I deserve" and is musically accompanied with soft pads in the back. This is followed by Parveen singing the next few lines while a tabla groove without the drums plays on that gives it the traditional vibe and a break from the electro-synthetic soundscape presented in the chorus. This eventually leads to the main refrain once again with the electronic rhythmic groove re-introduced, but this time it extends until the end of the song for around two minutes with a chordal progression suited for an outro section of a song. The line "Tu Jhoom" is sung repeatedly by the backing vocalists while Parveen sings the rest of her lines in an improvised manner not bound by any rhythmic pattern, with Lal eventually joining in with hers in the same manner. The blend between the two unique voices is effortless and logical, with Parveen's thick vocal timbre covering the lower and middle registers and Lal's energetic and bright vocal texture occupying the higher registers or octaves of the song.

The video for "Tu Jhoom" was also a departure from the typical format of Coke Studio's past thirteen seasons. Directed by Zeeshan Parvez, a veteran music video director for Coke Studio as well as a musician himself, "Tu Jhoom" is visually

Abida Parveen in her element
Naseebo Lalsings "Tu Jhoom"

Backing Vocalist on Set
Dancers in Action

stunning, and contains references to both the Mughal era as well as Sufi sensibilities, with the quintessential Islamic lattice screens known as *jaalis* that give way to a bright gold light. The video completely fits with the specific vision and concept for the song. The opening shot begins with the Coke Studio logo glimmering in white amongst a dark setting, followed by a group of dancers standing with their arms slowly rising. The set resembles a hall of a Mughal palace, adorned with hanging lanterns and glimmering *diya* lamps all around. Lal is introduced first, seated atop a riser, singing her lines. Once she begins singing "Tu Jhoom," the cameraman pans to a musician playing a *surmandal*, followed by Abida Parveen sitting on a separate riser with headphones on, and a lyric stand placed in front of her as she sings her lines in her typically awe-inspiring manner. When the chorus kicks in, shots of the whirling dancers in green outfits come in sporadically, as well as shots of the backing choir clad in white dresses.

Groovy Lament from Lyari

In contrast to "Tu Jhoom" and its celebration of two of the most iconic and seasoned vocalists in Pakistan, Season 14's second release, "Kana Yaari," celebrates three young and aspiring vocalists stemming from the province of Balochistan and the region of Lyari, Karachi's most densely populated and sometimes volatile locale which is perceived by some as a "no-go" area due to the prevalence of a lot of disputing gangs. This track became the song that defines Coke Studio's original vision, creating an inclusive space for regional musicians and songwriters to collaborate together and create entirely unique compositions. The three artists sing in three entirely different genres. Kaifi Khaleel, who is now one of Pakistan's most popular singer/songwriters with his highly successful song "Kahani Suno 2.0," sings ballads in Urdu and Balochi. Then there is Eva B, a young female rapper with a fiercely independent, culturally unique flow which is a rare sight in Pakistan's and specifically Balochistan's somewhat conservative customs. Finally, the song features Wahab Bugti, a folk musician renowned for singing in Balochi and Urdu whilst playing the *danbura,* an indigenous plucked stringed instrument widely played in Balochi and Sindhi folk music. Bugti was one of the many Pakistanis left homeless by the 2022 floods that displaced nearly eight million people in the country.

Lyrically, the song, which was composed by Khalil and written by all three artists, is about treachery and the misuse of love. In Khalil's own words: "This is what I think about life—a person should stick to what he says and have transparency. What he is on the inside is what he should be on the outside. This is the reason I wrote this song, to reflect this reality. Some lyrics are about the *haalat* (situation) in Lyari, the way we are spending our lives there. I wanted to take all I've seen and experienced to put it into words" (Haleem, 2022).

Despite the somewhat melancholic and somber tone of the lyrical element of the song, Kana Yaari sonically emanates feelings of joy and celebration due to the direction taken by Xulfi and Abdullah Siddiqui, who again is the co-music producer of the song. The music begins with the strum of the *danbura* played by Bugti, clad in his traditional Balochi attire sitting on a table, who then begins singing the main refrain "Kana Yaari, Ghadaari …" in his raw and rustic voice. Immediately after his part ends, the *danbura* stops and the beat kicks in with an electronic kick drum, played flawlessly by Veteran drummer Kami Paul, a regular part of Coke Studio as a house band member since season 9, along with sporadic electronic effects coming in and out that sets the tone for the rest of the song. In comes Kaifi Khali with the first verse, and the moment he sings the first line, one can feel the emotional pull of his voice: a mixture of pain, youthfulness, and restraint. After a few lines of his verses, the synth bass pad is introduced, and the balalaika, played beautifully by Mairah Khan, comes in with a plucked arpeggio movement in spurts. Once the main refrain "Kana Yaari" begins, everything comes together, and the sound becomes robust along with an infectious rhythmic groove that one can't help dancing to.

Once the chorus ends, Eva B is introduced with her rap monologue. Her energetic and powerful voice along with her feisty delivery of the words, all sung in Balochi, blends in well with the overall theme of the song. Furthermore, the juxtaposition of quick-paced and aggressive rap, which is usually a male-dominated genre, with a burka-clad young woman from Balochistan, is incredible. After her part, Kaifi is re-introduced by singing the bridge, followed by Bugti who sings the second verse which is melodically the same as the first one but with different words. The arrangement, albeit simple, is effective and coherent, and in Rakae's opinion, that is what makes this song connect with its audience.

The video was directed by Jamal Rehman, who dazzles the audience with his brilliant use of continuous motion throughout the visual depiction of the song. The vibrant colors of the set as well as the style and outfits of all the musicians involved make for a memorable visual experience and give each individual in the video a unique identity that stays with the audience. Although his treatment of the visuals heavily contrasts with the lyrical theme of the song, the video perfectly fits with the groovy vibe of the music and remains true to the cultural identity each artist embodies.

Rehman mentions how he had to capture the lyrical message of the song, which was primarily about relationships, and related aspects of his own life vis-à-vis relationships, to his approach. He mentions three key elements to his approach; the first being the theatricality of the limitation of the format, the second being the idea of impressions that are created when you meet new people, and the third being the artists themselves. Hence, he came up with the idea that the set itself represents the musicians' personality, and each room within the set is a facet of that personality, and as you get to know the person, all these layers open up. This is why during the video, as the artists step into different rooms, the background colors of those rooms change accordingly with the lyrical content and flow of the song.

Ballad of the Superstars

Coke Studio 14's third track, "Sajan Das Na" (Lover Tell Me) features two of Pakistan's most popular vocalists, Atif Aslam and Momina Mustehsan. Atif Aslam has been a longtime superstar in Pakistan, rising to fame in the early 2000s with his super-hit song "Aadat," which became the first viral song to break the internet back then. Aslam has had quite a few extremely successful hits from Coke Studio, such as his rendition of the qawwali "Tajdar-e-Haram" from Season 8 and his remix of his own song "Jalpari" from Season 2.

Mustehsan, on the other hand, gained popularity in 2016 after she had her Coke Studio debut singing alongside Rahat Fateh Ali Khan on the song "Afreen Afreen." She has since then been featured multiple times on the show, and has many hit songs to her name, and some not-so-hit songs as well. Mustehsan's version of "Ko ko Karina" from her duet with actor Ahad Raza Mir in Season 11 received terrible reviews and reactions from both critics and listeners across the country, to the point where Pakistan's former minister for human rights, Shireen Mazari, chimed in and called the song "horrendous" and a "massacre" on the social media platform X (formerly known as Twitter). This is due to the fact that they tried to replicate a very popular classic pop song from the 1960s that was originally sung by Ahmed Rushdie, in almost exactly the same way sonically as it was produced back then, with an added air of inauthenticity as showcased in their very retro costumes.

Nonetheless, Mustehsan has remained a Coke Studio regular, while Ahad Raza Mir has seemingly decided to stick to acting.

"Sajan Das Na" was the first collaborative song between Mustehsan and Aslam, and certainly was much anticipated by listeners worldwide. Produced once again by Abdullah Siddiqui and written by Adnan Dhool and Mustehsan, the song is a lament about how two lovers cannot be together due to the effects of fame and fortune. The song received mixed reviews from critics and listeners, as their expectations may have exceeded what the song actually is, a rather okay pop-ballad sung by two veteran Coke Studio artists. According to an article in the Pakistani daily *Dawn Images*, "Another user felt the song was 'meh', especially after 'Tu Jhoom' and 'Kana Yari'" (2022).

Whilst the song follows a similar format in terms of soundscape to that of the other two releases, "Sajan Das Na" has a melody that sits on an electronic percussive groove that is close to Western R&B music and does not deviate much from that style of music. The song begins with a soft melodic line played by the harp accompanied by a two-chord progression. It gives a fitting introduction to Aslam singing the first verse with the beat kicking in, all the while looking at the part he is supposed to be embodying, with his hair slicked back, and an all-leather outfit accessorized with gold chains. If the visuals are supposed to add to the emotions and narrative of the songs—and we know that is true for this season—then this visual absolutely emanates that chill, laid-back, almost sensual energy of a classic R&B song.

In fact, as Aslam reaches the chorus, we get to hear Mustehsan joining in with breathy single liners. That coupled with the bold reds, moody purples, and cool blues of the background set really drives the sensuality of this song home.

The next verse is sung by Mustehsan, who is wearing a very becoming fusion outfit featuring a pantsuit with a *desi* motif, coupled with a traditional South Asian choker style necklace. The melody of her verses also feels more South Asian femme fatale, in contrast with Aslam's suave slick crooning. While both are very talented singers, the song remains unmemorable compared to the rest of the tracklist of the season.

A Soulful Melancholic Melody of Soothing Voices

The fourth release of Season 14 is a song called "Mehram," which featured two of Pakistan's most soulful vocalists currently. The first is Arooj Aftab, who is originally from Lahore but is now based in New York, and made headlines for being the first Pakistani to win a Grammy in 2022. The second artist is the versatile vocalist Asfar Hussain, who is from Chitral, and is also a lead member of the band Bayaan, a progressive alternative rock band that won Pepsi's music show called "Pepsi Battle of the Bands" in 2017. Their song together is titled "Mehram," which literally means spouse, and is a song about a person expressing his heartache at the loss of his beloved. In this song, Coke Studio offers the listeners an original and penetratingly haunting piece of music. The pairing of Aftab and Hussain was wonderful, as they both have soothing and soulful voices that perfectly suit the songs' vibe. In addition, both artists have a reputation for singing songs that are similarly melancholic and sensuous in nature.

A brief background of both vocalists is necessary. Arooj Aftab skyrocketed to fame after becoming the first Pakistani to win a Grammy Award for Best Global Performance for her original rendition of her song "Mohabbat" in 2022 as well as being nominated for the "Best New Artist" category during the same year. It was an incredible achievement for the aspiring vocalist who has been a regular performer and music producer in the United States since the last fifteen years or so when she permanently shifted to New York on her own. Before moving to New York, Aftab had gotten admission into Berklee College of Music in Boston where she earned a double degree in music engineering and production. Following that, she steadily built her career as a solo artist and released three albums titled *Bird under Water*, *Siren Islands*, and *Vulture Prince*. In 2022, she also gave a stellar performance at the Coachella festival which features some of the world's most renowned artists and bands and is considered a highly prestigious event for music globally. She has also collaborated and produced for world-renowned sitar player and composer Anoushka Shankar, who is the daughter of the late sitar maestro Pandit Ravi Shankar.

Asfar Hussain, a vocalist similar in style to Aftab, has been performing in the Pakistani music industry consistently over the last decade or so. He has been a lead member of the band Bayaan since its inception and made a huge impact with their first two songs "Farda" and "Nahein Milta" which were initially released on Soundcloud, primarily due to their sophisticated Urdu lyrics and Asfar's soft but assertive vocal tone and intricate singing style. In 2016 and 2017, he sang a few songs for Nescafe Basement, which was produced by Xulfi as well, for which he received critical acclaim and made his mark as one of Pakistan's top vocalists. In 2018, Hussain and his band won the Pepsi Battle of the Bands competition. Since then, Hussain has released two studio albums with Bayaan titled *Suno* and *4 Saal*, and has several singles released as well.

The song "Mehram," which was yet again produced by Abdullah Siddiqui, begins with a minimal soundscape with layers of ambient synth pads. Hussain begins the song with a verse, accompanied with a chordal progression played on the piano, along with a cocktail of reversed sonic samples that perfectly sets the tone of the song. Once the main line "Tu Mehram" begins, a low bass tone enters with a melodic phrase played on the cello. The emptiness brings out the character exceptionally well. Once Hussain's part ends, a minimal beat begins with Aftab's soft vocals coming into play. The music slowly builds with the beat, the cello, and the piano until both vocalists sing the main chorus line together. The melancholic yet beautiful and intricate soundscape then perfectly flows into the chorus singing chant-like phrases that bring all the music together. The song primarily continues in this method until the last minute of the song, where the intensity of violins and the string section increases in volume and expression.

A Punjabi Wedding Groove

The first few seconds of Coke Studio Season 14's fifth song, "Neray Neray Vas," are enough to convince you that this song will make you want to dance. The song is performed by sufi-rock duo Soch The Band, which consists of Adnan Dhool and Rabi Ahmed, as well as Shamroz Butt and Umair Butt who are known as the Butt Brothers. "Neray Neray Vas," which is Punjabi for "Come close to me," is a remake of Soch's 2016 song by the same name. Sung in Punjabi, it follows a familiar trope of a lover trying to convince her partner of her undying love for him, and earnestly requesting him to return that love back to her by always being close to her.

In addition to singing this song, Adnan Dhool was also one of the associate music producers of Season 14, and is an exceptional lyricist as well. Dhool is known for his robust vocal delivery and for his unique folksy composition style. He made quite an impact with his song "Bol Hu" featured in Nescafe Basement in 2019—again produced by Xulfi—which was a collaboration with young aspiring female vocalist Hadiya Hashmi, and was received with critical acclaim in Pakistan.

As "Neray Neray Vas" begins, the delicate plucking of the tumbi, played by Haider Ali compels you to start tapping your feet along as Adnan Dhool begins to sing. The smooth synth introduced by Zain Ali stands in sweet juxtaposition with the more traditionally South Asian instruments like the soft dholak played by Asif Ali, as well as Veeru Shan's *matka* and *chimta*, hinting to the listener that this is another one of Coke Studio's trademark fusion songs. The matka is a ceramic vase-like vessel typically used for carrying and storing water. However, when it is empty, striking the belly creates sounds ranging from warm, hollow thumps, to sharp, earthy thuds, depending on where you strike it. The chimta on the other hand is a metal tong-like percussive instrument that produces a shimmering metallic clang when the two prongs are struck together. The two percussive instruments, along with the rich, deep drums of the dholak, stand in contrast to the cool, electronic synth sounds in "Neray Neray Vas." What do you get when you add pop synth elements to an otherwise traditionally tumbi, harmonium, and dholak-filled Punjabi song? The next big dance number of course. And the dance floor is precisely where "Neray Neray Vas" transports you as soon as the chorus hits.

Any reluctance to dance is completely eradicated by the time the Butt Brothers enter the song. Immediately after the chorus, we get a Punjabi rap by the brothers accentuated by the sassy beat of the dholak backed up by the tumbi and the harmonium. Shamroz Butt and Umair Butt, who go by the name Butt Brothers are, in fact, biological brothers who have been working as producers for some local rappers. This is their breakthrough song, and for good reason. They bring life to the song, aurally as well as physically, as throughout the accompanying music video, they can be seen dancing along to the song, hands up in the air, just two seconds away from breaking out into a proper bhangra.

The video, directed by Murtaza Niaz, also plays into the idea of the song's potential to be the wedding song of the season by choosing a color palette full of reds and oranges, set to moody red lighting reflected in pools of water. The ensemble around the three singers chimes in with bhangra appropriate *hoye hoye's*, and by the end of the song, everyone is laughing and swaying along to the music while they play their respective instruments.

As far as remakes go, Dhool and the Butt Brothers successfully enhanced the overall impact of the song as it raised the tempo of the original song and made it less of a softer ballad and more of an energetic upbeat dance number. The song was very well received by Pakistani audiences and made its way into many dance sequences and *mehndi* events this year during Pakistan's wedding season.

An Anthem for the Marginalized

The sixth song off of Coke Studio Season 14 hardly needs an introduction, on account of its overwhelming success and critical acclaim. The song titled "Pasoori," performed by singer-songwriter Ali Sethi and newcomer Shae Gill, became an overnight hit, reaching impressive milestones such as being the first Pakistani song to be featured on Spotify's "Viral 50—Global" chart, and being the world's most searched song in 2022, accordion to Google's "Year in Search Trends" report. The song currently has 696 million views on YouTube, making it the most-watched Coke Studio music video of all time.

Written by Ali Sethi and Fazal Abbas, the song is said to have been penned by the former during a time when Pakistani and Indian performers were not allowed to partake in gigs across the border. Sethi has said that he found inspiration for one of the key lines of the song from a quote written on the back of a local truck. While the song outwardly seems to be a straightforward love song about two lovers lamenting over the distance between them, a closer reading bespeaks an undercurrent of angst and a playful commentary on the politics between India and Pakistan and their own "star-crossed love."

Aurally, the song is a very intentional blend of musical styles, borrowing elements from traditional Punjabi folk songs, to reggaeton beats and almost flamenco inspired claps.

Associate Music Producer Abdullah Siddiqui in an official press release described the song as "a groundbreaking new hybrid genre [...] one of the most modern tracks of the season." In fact, this ethnically ambiguous, uber-global aesthetic is carried over into the visuals of the music video as well. We see Sethi dressed in a West African inspired *kurta pajama* set, while Gill dons a flowy white dress with a colorful vest embroidered with traditional motifs, looking effortlessly bohemian with arms bearing a rainbow of bangles and hair that is styled in a loose and flowing manner. The set, designed by Lahore-based art director Hashim Ali, resembles the sort of central courtyard you would see in a typical *haveli* in Old Lahore, but with an explosion of colors. The video also features the famed Bharatanatyam dancer, Sheema Kermani, dressed in bright sunny yellow.

The song starts with a synth-heavy overture, coupled with Kermani's graceful dance. As the overture fades out, a series of claps lead us into the actual beat of the song, and Sethi begins his plea in his soft dulcet voice. "I'll set fire to your compulsions / to the sticky mess of waiting, coming and going," he sings, addressing a lover who promised to come, but ended up not coming. He leads us into the chorus, where he chides his lover for not being able to know how the distance between them affects him.

Soon after, Shae Gill's mature, soulful vocals take over the next verse. The depth of her voice is reminiscent of old Punjabi folk singers, and it is very easy to forget that this is her debut performance. The highlight of the song is the bridge, where Sethi and Gill's voices blend perfectly as they reach a truly festive crescendo, urging their lovers to run away with them. "Give me life, give me love, take me in your arms" they sing in a passionate frenzy.

The viral success of "Pasoori" is reflected in the fact that *The New Yorker* dedicated an entire article to the song in 2022, holding it responsible for "uniting India and Pakistan." The article, written by Indian-American author Priyanka Mattoo, drew a fair amount of ire from some Pakistanis, who felt that in the current political climate between the two neighboring countries, it was a stretch and an injustice to say that a popular song had "united" the nations and healed all long-standing grievances, especially during a time when India's right-wing Hindu nationalist leadership had given cover to the marked rise in sectarian violence. The article was also criticized for ignoring the role of Sethi's privilege in his musical success, as he is the son of politician Jugnu Mohsin and well-connected journalist Najam Sethi, and in general belongs to a very prominent family. Another critique of the article was that it did not give Shae Gill enough credit, especially considering the fact that she had instantly become one of the biggest new voices in music, representing not just women but also the Christian minority of Pakistan.

Journalistic hyperbole aside, the metrics speak for themselves. In fact, in June 2023, the song was remade for an Indian film, where it was performed by Indian singer and composer Arijit Singh. In the piece for *The New Yorker*, Sethi was quoted as saying that he had wanted to make a "banger" after witnessing the reception "bedroom-pop" artists like Hassan Raheem had been getting. If that was indeed his wish, it was definitely granted, as "Pasoori" was definitely the most successful song of Coke Studio's Season 14.

"Pasoori's" success can also be attributed to the vibrant visual aesthetic created by director Kamal Khan and production designer Hashmi Ali. Both individuals had aptly captured the essence of the song, which focuses on acceptance, diversity, and celebrating the creativity within the artists, dancers, and characters within the song. According to journalist Maheen Sabeeh's article titled "The 'Pasoori' Phenomenon" (2022), Hashim Ali had "created a communal space where artists can celebrate every dimension of humanity—not just through ethnicity, but also through variety in emotion, style and spirituality." This precisely falls in line with Xulfi's and the executive producers' vision of Season 14. In Rakae's conversation with Abdullah Siddiqui, when asked about the reason for the success of "Pasoori," he mentions, "It was the perfect storm. What Kamal and Hashim did visually, was to present a new syntax of South Asian Art that took South Asian-ness on a global level. They've created this space and built an actual neighborhood," he said, continuing, "So, people who watch that want to be there, they want to be part of that party, where you have all these different people dancing, and all these different styles and all these little pockets of space with different characters with different identities. It's a world, and it's world building."

A Hard Rock and Rap Combo

Metal isn't the most accessible or approachable genre of music in Pakistan, so it makes sense that for Coke Studio's seventh song, the nu-metal anthem "Ye Dunya" (This World), they paired alternative metal band Karakoram with rappers Talha Anjum and Faris Shafi. The song was conceived by Karakoram vocalist Sherry Khattak and Coke Studio producer Xulfi, who also wrote it alongside Adnan Dhool, Anjum, and Shafi.

In true metal fashion, the song is an angsty anthem that decries the materialism and isolation of this world, coming to the eventual conclusion that we are not alone. Right off the bat it starts with an emotional declaration from Karakoram front-man Sherry Khattak, who claims that the world does not stop for anyone, and it keeps going forward as people keep coming into and going out of your life. The set for the accompanying video is intentionally kept dark and dimly lit, in order to really drive the angst home. Khattak and his fellow Karakoram members all stand in individual box-like structures, which highlight the song's theme of isolation and desolation. We get a brief glimpse of an orchestra of violins, which adds to the drama. To that end, music journalist and engineer Zeerak Ahmed writes in his newsletter Hamnawa, "There are so many things to love about this song beyond its construction. The existentialism of its theme, the brutalist architecture of the set, the star-making of Talha Anjum and Faris Shafi. Anjum and Karakoram's fatalist feel is a perfect fit" (2022).

The video then pans out to reveal Talha Anjum standing on a platform in front of what looks to be a construction site. The platform lights up and we get a moody strobe show of green and blue lights as Anjum begins to rap. Anjum has been lauded for his introspective, thought-provoking raps, and is best known for being one half of the rap duo Young Stunners, who have also been featured on this season of Coke Studio. His philosophical musings shine through in this song, with him reflecting on his own journey of sadness which "continued to be nurtured in his heart, from darkness to light, from flaw to silence." Anjum concedes that God is endlessly generous, and then proceeds to ask Him to be less generous when it comes to Anjum's pain and suffering.

As Anjum comes to the realization that even if he feels like he is alone, he always has God by his side, the visuals of the video also take a turn and start introducing more color courtesy of augmented reality images by Zeeshan Parwez, one of Pakistan's leading music video directors, signaling a shift in tone of the song. This is further cemented by Faris Shafi's section of the song. If Anjum's rap was softer and more introspective, Shafi's is the exact opposite with razor-sharp explicitness and self-assuredness. However, it was felt by some that Shafi may have toned down his entertainingly acerbic tongue a bit too much in an act of self-censorship of the sort that is required by Coke Studio, as per *The Express Tribune* (2022). Nonetheless, Shafi and his very obvious self-confidence and wit still force you to pay attention to him, whether you like it or not.

The most exciting part of the song in Khadija's opinion was Annan Naukhez's guitar solo that really heightened the drama and tension of the song. The solo is supported by the violin orchestra; however, the violins get drowned during the solo, which could have really benefited from more prominent violins, as the layering of a loud, tormented electric guitar, with piercing, almost anxious violins would have been wonderfully cinematic and dramatic. Nonetheless, the climatic solo does a good job at really highlighting the contrast that follows when everything quietens down and Khattak takes over the mic once again. The song ends with Khattak giving us one good solid scream as we are played out by the soft violins and a reminder by Anjum that we are not alone.

A Melodic Banger with an Attitude

Coke Studio Season 14's eighth song had uniquely piqued Khadija's interest. The song, titled "Peechay Hutt" (Get Back), featured Pakistani sweetheart Hasan Raheem and producer extraordinaire Talal Qureshi in collaboration with the Justin Bibis, who were the reason for her interest. For the uninitiated, unaware, and just plain ignorant, "Justin Bibis" was the name given to Muqadaran Tabeydar and Sania Sohail, two sisters who went viral in 2015 for their cover of Justin Bieber's song "Baby." The video, which was uploaded to YouTube nearly eight years ago, featured the two young girls on a street in Lahore, singing Bieber's hit song "Baby," while their mother provided percussion by playing beats on a small metal pot. The video spread like wildfire, and the sisters were catapulted into fame, being interviewed by the BBC, and even being featured in the ICC World Cup 2015 anthem. They also worked with producers on creating soundtracks for TV serials, but none of them had seemed to make a huge impact. Khadija had been trying to get in touch with them or their manager, in a bid to profile them and see what they were up to now, since they had slipped under the radar since 2015. The chance to rediscover them was finally presented after their breakthrough performance in the fourteenth season of Coke Studio.

The first hint of what to expect from the song comes from the opening visuals. We see a hand drop a coin into a blue coin slit set against a colorful backdrop of neon colors, and then a video game menu pops up, with little avatars of Raheem, Qureshi, and the Justin Bibis. Immediately, a groovy bassline is introduced followed by a thumping beat as Raheem gets ready to jump into his bit. The 1970s-esque neon colors, cold blue city lights in the background, and the glitchy visual effects add to the very electronic, very retro but also futuristic feel of the song.

Raheem begins delivering his verses in his signature smooth dulcet voice, with the ease and effortlessness of someone who has been doing this for a while. Interestingly, Raheem's decision to include some verses in Shina, which is the language spoken in Gilgit-Baltistan and Chitral, really resonated with a lot of listeners, who were happy at the linguistic representation. Coke Studio is certainly no stranger to incorporating major regional languages in their songs; but the subtle incorporation of a less prominent language in a song featuring some relatively newer and younger musicians was a welcome choice.

Of course, most welcome of all was the choice to diversify the kind of music being released this season, and "Peechay Hutt" is one of the biggest examples of this choice. The upbeat groovy synth-pop song is not what Coke Studio usually goes for and is a departure from the quintessential Coke Studio folk song cover template. Perhaps it is for this reason that the song left many people divided, as reported by *Dawn Images*, which said, "There were some netizens who weren't into the song and were confused about Raheem choosing to 'do this to himself'" (2022).

Nonetheless, people were very into Justin Bibis's portion of the song, and truthfully, it might be the most memorable moment. Muqadaran and Sania's raw soulful voices perfectly cut the smoothness of Raheem's and added some much needed and very welcome character and sass to the otherwise straightforward song.

The synth melody looping through the song is very bouncy and almost playful, which is a nice call back to the visuals at the start of the song, as well as the gaming arcade vibe of the set. The addition of the beat really adds life to the song, and helps highlight the raw character in the voices of the two sisters. This is definitely one of those ear-wormy kind of songs that will get stuck in your head and randomly pop up in situations where you're not looking for an infectious song to make you bop your head along to.

Coke Studio itself describes the song as a "flashpoint for a new generation's rise," which, while slightly hyperbolic, is somewhat true. If not the rise of a new generation altogether, it at least is heralding the dawn of a new era in Coke Studio history. In this new era, newcomers, indie musicians, forgotten viral sensations, and alternative genres can find a space for themselves. It does very much signal a directorial shift and promises to keep things enterprising.

A Powerhouse Anthem from the Shafi Siblings

Faris and Meesha Shafi are a dynamic sibling duo with incredibly distinct and well-regarded musical careers. When Coke Studio put them together for Season 14's song "Muazaz Saarif" (respected customer), many wondered what that would sound like, sonically. On one hand you have a fiery, sultry, Punjabi powerhouse in Meesha, while in Faris you have a feisty, witty, sharp-tongued rapper. And while Punjabi rap is certainly not a new idea, the distinct personalities of both musicians could have very well made it a risky gamble. But that was not the case. "Muazziz Saarif" works because of the one important thing the siblings have in common: explosiveness.

The song begins with the slow plucks of a mono synth that almost sounds like a ticking clock, adding to the buildup and anticipation of what is to follow. And what is to follow is a bass drop that announces Faris's entry. The rapper is fast, he is clean, and he is sharp. It is immediately clear that hello, it is indeed Faris on the mic, as he launches a spitfire of what can only be described as aggressive self-love combined with a classic diss track toward his competitors. Declaring that he is "better than medicine," he dismisses his competition's songs as "repetitive," claiming that they "go into hiding" whenever he's on a mission. All of this takes place over a constant background of an ebbing bass and a beat—and not much else, adding to the drama of the song.

Instead of building up to a bass drop that leads to the chorus, the song takes a different route. It slows down, following which Meesha comes in, slow and haunting, not unlike a siren song. It feels very much like the calm before the storm as a *tabla* bass drop, courtesy of Joshua Amjad, precedes the songstress taking the song to a fiery climax. And indeed, this fiery burst of energy is also addressed in her verses, with her claiming that she is a tempest—"mein aandhi mein haneri"—"I am a windstorm, I am a tornado." She continues the theme of self-love in a tone less aggressive than her brother's by saying that whatever she says, comes from the heart, but the world can't handle it. The chorus ends with Meesha advising the listener to forge their own new path, lest they end up getting lost in the rat race of the world.

Visually, the song echoes the intensity of its message, with the set being modeled to look like the interior of a classy, elegant mansion, with red and golden hued chandeliers, wooden paneled and wallpapered walls, and big stained glass windows that give it an almost church hall like feel. The "house" feels very art-deco, and this is reiterated in not just the geometric wallpaper, but also in Meesha's costuming, with her donning a 1920s-esque pearl headpiece coupled with a modern twist on the traditional saari.

While the song's messaging stands true for everyone as far as general concepts go, when viewed against Meesha's own battles with sexism and how the public has perceived and treated her, it becomes an interesting and powerful social commentary. In 2018, Meesha filed a case with the Punjab Ombudsman, a faction of the provincial government that is mandated to resolve cases of workplace harassment against women, alleging that veteran pop singer Ali Zafar had sexually harassed her. Since then, there has been a lot of legal back-and-forth on the case, but most damagingly, fans of Ali Zafar—who has alleged that Shafi lied about the harassment in order to obtain a Canadian citizenship—have used this as a way to denounce the #MeToo movement in Pakistan. The case remains unresolved as of yet.

Following the chorus, Faris takes up the mic again, this time supported by a background chorus of trumpet-like synths, which cements the song as an assertive anthem. It's almost reminiscent of the sass in American rapper Macklemore's hit song "Thrift Shop." His quick witticisms are followed by Meesha performing the bridge and the final chorus, where she offers some social commentary by posing a rhetorical question. "How will you resist and control a rebellious spirit? How many kinds of molds will you shape us in?" she asks in the bridge, with those same soft haunting vocals from the pre-chorus. With this sagacious advice, we build up to the final chorus of the song, with booming bass, raging trumpets, and Meesha's fiery admittance to being a tempest.

A Song about Being Carefree

Momina Mustehsan's "Beparwah" was the only solo song on this season of Coke Studio. It was also Mustehsan's second song of the season, and sonically, both songs couldn't be more different. Where "Sajjan Das Na" was a groovy R&B inspired upbeat song, "Beparwah" is a soft, soulful plea to God, a familiar theme for Coke Studio, which historically hasn't yet shied away from adopting the more internationally acceptable Sufi-music identity. The song was written and composed by Adnan Dhool along with co-authorship and composition by Mustehsan, showrunner Xulfi and Rabi Ahmed. Xulfi and Action Zain were once again responsible for the arrangement and production of the song.

Accurately described by the show as an "intimate conversation," the song opens with the gentle beating of faraway drums and the dulcet plucking of the sarod, played masterfully by Muzamil Husain. Not long after, Mustehsan implores to the Divine, claiming that she has prayed and appealed to God to reunite her with her lover. The buildup to the chorus consists of rising synths, courtesy of Action Zain and Saad ul Hassan, that mimic the rising anxiety and agitation faced by someone who feels helpless as they beseech the Higher Powers to intervene. The drumbeats provided by Yusuf Ramay and Haroon Daniel very cleverly sound very much like a heartbeat, again adding to the heightened emotions of the song. The chorus sees Mustehsan asking God not to forsake her, begging him to not be upset with her for her wish to be reunited with her lover.

This is followed by a well-timed and somewhat sassy sounding harmonium interlude by Asad Ali, layered over tense synth rhythms, after which the song eases up and we get a beautiful sarod solo by Muzamil Husain. The sarod sounds delicate and gentle, and given the theme of the song, it almost sounds pleading in context. This interlude really makes the song as otherwise, it runs the risk of sounding too monotonous and dare we say, vanilla?

Visually, the set for "Beparwah" is dreamy, magical, and romantic. In the opening scene, we see Mustehsan sitting in a room teeming with plants, very reminiscent of a greenhouse. As she starts singing, she walks out of the room into a vast forest, dimly lit as if by moonlight. If this is a metaphor for how our emotional and mental crises can amplify a minor issue into a behemoth, then it is very successful. As the songstress wanders through the forest, we see a lot of the musicians dispersed throughout, some perched on the ground, leaning against a tree, others standing with their instruments. Somewhere along the journey we encounter a choir that joins and supports Mustehsan's plea, really hitting the religious undertones of the song on the nose. The closing visual is Mustehsan's silhouette sitting alone in the forest, as she gazes out at a starlit sky.

A Funky Devotional Sonic Delight

"Thagyan" is the eleventh track on Coke Studio Season 14, and as such, it is one of the few songs this season that feel very reminiscent of the "old" Coke Studio. Performed by brothers Zain and Zohaib Ali, who go by Zain Zohaib, and vocal powerhouse Quratulain Baloch, the song is a more upbeat reimagining of the traditional qawwali. The song was written by Zain and Zohaib along with Asim Raza, and was composed, arranged, and produced by Action Zain and Xulfi.

"Thagyan" begins with a perky beat supported by the plucking of the tumbi, played by Haider Ali. As Melvin Arthur introduces a strong, brooding synth bassline, Zohaib begins his lament in his deep raspy voice. Thematically, the song is a playful complaint to a lover for being hard-to-get but very easy to want. In the official press release for the song, associate producer Action Zain said he had wanted to strip the qawwali down to the bare minimum, and then "reinflate it" by adding tablas, dholaks, and supporting qawwals, known as *humnawa*. The toned-down qawwali works well; the result is an upbeat, fresh twist on a beloved form of music. Many listeners have used the word "playful" to describe the song online, as noted by Dawn Images.

Zain and Zohaib's raspy voices mesh well with Quratulain Baloch's "sandpapery" vocals (*The Express Tribune*), and all three performers complement each other's energy. Baloch's voice is raw and rife with emotion; it is not difficult to believe that she really is protesting against the trickery of a lover. The addition of the wonderful and warm brass section, conducted by Nijaat Sahab and comprising Basharat Ali, Mehboob Hussain, Muhammad Aslam, and Riaz Ahmed, is what really elevates the song and takes it into an almost sassy feel, while highlighting the more modern elements of what is essentially a timeless *qawwali.*

The beats remain subtle, the bass drops are never boisterous, and just when you think the solos are getting repetitive and the percussion seems to be monotonous, either a brass section is introduced or a new vocal section is initiated to create a constantly moving and vivid song that takes you on a journey.

Visually, the song has the signature Coke Studio red neon lights that surge throughout the song. This too, contributes to the illusion of a return to the Coke Studio of yore, one that was characterized by a neon-lit studio where all the performers were situated in a circle, jamming together while facing each other. As we watch Baloch and the Ali brothers sway to the rhythm of the music, completely in a world of their own, and we watch the musicians smile and nod at each other while they dance in place, it feels very familiar and comfortable, which is the success of the song.

Let's Go!

The penultimate song of Coke Studio Season 14, called "Go," was described in the official press release as a dreamy hyperpop "ode to sensitivity" performed by Abdullah Siddiqui and Atif Aslam, who also composed it along with rapper Rehman Asfar, better known by his stage name Maanu. Siddiqui and Maanu also wrote the song along with Xulfi, who aided in the production as well.

The song opens with a cinematic string section courtesy of David Joseph, which feels even more dramatic as it is set over computer-generated visuals of galaxies and star clusters that we pan away from to reveal a house filled with gentle pink clouds. This dreamscape of a house is where Siddique and Aslam and the musicians are situated, and it is from here that we get pulled in by the sharp and rich sound of the sarangi being played by Gul Muhammad. Juxtaposing the very Punjabi sounds of the sarangi is an array of modern percussive instruments, giving the song that signature Coke Studio fusion.

Also adding to the fusion is the fact that lyrically, it's a mixture of English and Urdu. Siddique, who sings primarily in English, croons in his soft velvety voice, admitting to his own sentimentality. The camera then pans to Aslam, who is lounging on a nearby recliner, perched in front of big windows that look out deep into space. Aslam sings in Urdu and is able to match Siddiqui's energy quite well. Although it can be a bit jarring to see him join in on the English verses, especially as he doesn't ordinarily sing in English, he doesn't seem too out of place. He certainly looks the part, dressed in a colorful hoodie and track pants, which is a departure from his more usual look, as well as his getup in the previously discussed song "Sajjan Das Na" which he also performed this season, alongside Momina Mustehsan.

With Waqas Hussain on the sitar, and a background symphony of synth, the chorus reads as another self-love anthem. "I knew it from the get-go / Ke naheen hu kamzor" (I am not weak) sing Siddiqui and Aslam in unison. Even though lyrically it isn't the strongest song of the season, the youthful energy and pomp that the song exudes make up for the shortcomings. It's not what one would have expected from a collaboration between Aslam and Siddiqui, but perhaps that is the whole point.

Halfway through the song, a fog-machine has turned the already dreamy set into a hazy tranquil daze. What really elevates the dreamscape aspect of the song, and is made most apparent during the second verse, is the mechanical, almost computer-like beeps and chirps courtesy of the synths. It's a very Adbullah Siddiqui thing to do, and it really elevates the song. The futuristic sounding production coupled with Urdu lyrics and the traditional *tabla* and sarangi makes "Go" a very interesting example of a Pakistani hyper-pop song.

Until We Meet Again

The thirteenth and final episode of Coke Studio Season 14 features a collaboration between venerated singer Faisal Kapadia of Strings fame and Talha Anjum and Talha Yunus of Young Stunners. The song "Phir Milenge" (we will meet again) was written by Young Stunners and Adnan Dhool, with additional lyrics by Xulfi, who also composed and produced it alongside Abdullah Siddiqui.

Thematically, "Phir Milenge" is about "memories," according to the official Coke Studio press release accompanying the song. It was described as a song about someone who has left your life, but still remains in your heart and soul, but it also works as being a promise from Coke Studio to return again next year, as the song closes the season.

The video for "Phir Milenge" was skillfully directed and shot in one take by Zeeshan Parvaiz. The opening visuals showcase a window that looks out at various glitching scenes that morph into one another, changing from an open road surrounded by green fields to an orange hazy barbed wire wall, eventually landing on what it is: a green screen room. The music creeps in slowly, and it is limited to just a haunting synth and a very simple piano note. In the background we hear the soft rumbling of storm clouds, which give the song a dark, brooding atmosphere. Faisal Kapadia opens in his deep soulful voice, addressing the metaphorical ghost of a former lover, claiming to have still held onto memories of his lover in the back of his heart.

The video then pans out toward Talha Yunus who leads us through one corridor after the other. In fact, the music video, which was another one-take wonder by Zeeshan Parwez, features all three singers wandering through a dimly lit maze, never really intersecting with or meeting each other. While Yunus begins rapping, some percussion is added into the song, along with surging synths which add not just energy, but also an eerie air to the song.

The focus is then shifted to Anjum, and the percussion slows down to just a soft thumping, reminiscent of a heartbeat, which feels very at home, given the emotional confessional nature of the song. As Anjum beckons his lover to meet him, we hear warping synths played by Payam Mashrequi. "I got a lot of pain / Why can't I ever get you?" he asks. The rapper continues his sharp, emotional declaration, claiming that since the departure of his beloved, his house has stopped feeling like a home. By this point Yusuf Ramay and Haroon Daniel on the drums and octapad respectively have morphed the beat so that it sounds like a ticking clock.

The chorus has Kapadia delivering soul crushing lines such as "Bhoola nahi, mein bhi tujhay / Mere liye mein ne, sazaa rakhi hai" (I have also not forgotten you / For myself, I have kept a punishment). Immediately after, we get a haunting and bittersweet ensemble of violins and cellos, which amplifies the already emotional song. After another verse by Talha Yunus, the final chorus comes in, with Kapadia belting out the heartbreaking final lines. The video ends with him eventually finding his way out of the maze, walking into the sunlight, showing that maybe there is a way out of the misery after all.

"Phir Milengay" was a perfect choice to wrap up the season as it connotes how this is the beginning of many journeys ahead for Coke Studio and its listeners. It reminds the audience that the show, much like a phoenix, has risen from the ashes many times, and has always managed to come back.

Coke Studio's Great Comeback

Although Coke Studio had enjoyed a considerable amount of success in its nearly fifteen-year run in Pakistan, its luck had begun to run out by Season 10. It was around this time that underground musicians, indie artists, and music lovers in general began to notice flaws in the grand plan of the Coke Studio format. There are only so many times you can get high-profile artists to cover songs without bored audiences losing interest and aspiring musicians losing hope, which is precisely the curse that afflicted Coke Studio.

The complaints? For one, it was argued that the show hindered the production and appreciation of new, original music by making audiences accustomed to revamped covers. In a conversation Khadija had with Jamal Rehman in 2020, he explained that the consequences of Coke Studio's many song covers extend beyond just straightforward repetitiveness. In fact, because of the TV shows' popularity, coupled with a lack of the kind of infrastructure associated with a traditional music industry, Coke Studio, and by extension, the Coca-Cola company are actually controlling music tastes and preferences. The fear was that because the people had so far been enjoying the regurgitated song cover format, which in turn was drawing in revenue for the company, there would be no incentive to change course and introduce new music. Which is, if you think about it, a little ironic, considering that people eventually did lose interest, and the corporation was in fact forced to regroup and change its course.

To that effect, it was also feared that there would be no incentive to introduce new up-and-coming artists either. This was another widely held complaint aimed at Coke Studio, who up till then had been inviting already well-established and popular singers to their platform. By Season 10, critics had begun pointing out the need to introduce new voices to the platform. Journalist and academic Rafay Mahmood wrote for *The Express Tribune* that, "The biggest challenge for the show is to bridge the gap between the indie scene and the mainstream musicians." (2017). And certainly, the indie scene had, around this time, become less traditionally underground, and had made a mark on Pakistani audiences, especially the youth. Platforms like Facebook and YouTube made both sharing and accessing music easier, and music festivals like the Lahore Music Meet further publicized new artists, making their erasure from Coke Studio all the more noticeable. A review published in *The News* argued that "the most deserving musician who deserves to have a spot on the show is Mooroo, one of the most consistently original and prolific musicians Pakistan has seen in recent times. What about Abid Brohi and SomeWhatSuper? The two names have become a huge hit in Pakistan since '*The Sibbi Song*' and it would make sense to have them on board."

Coke Studio, in its fifteen-year run, has only strayed from its format twice. The first time was in 2018, when then-producers Ali Hamza and Zohaib Kazi introduced a spin-off series titled *Coke Studio Explorer*. The series had five episodes that followed the producers collaborating with unknown regional singers from five different regions of Pakistan, and was met with a lot of success and praise for its originality and attention to discovering new musical talent.

Coke Studio Season 14 is the second example of a major departure from the traditional Coke Studio format. For one, visually, this season was different from its predecessors. Gone was the dimly lit studio with neon red LED panels glowing in the back, and ornate traditional carpets covering the floors. Gone was the feeling of gatecrashing a private jam session between the country's biggest musical names covering the country's biggest musical hits. Gone also was the now tired Sufi, folk aesthetic of the show, visually and sonically. Instead, so focused was Season 14 on embracing the new, that not only did it completely do away with the old video format, but it also went a step further by giving each song a completely different video, with its own unique set and aesthetic.

As refreshing as it was for the audience, it also subliminally made the change in tone clear. Coke Studio would no longer stand being called "cover studio" or being seen as a glorified jam session between veteran musicians. Instead, it was now in the business of producing new music that catered to new audiences. The vice president of Coca-Cola Pakistan and Afghanistan said of this new music direction, "Whereas the values are the same, but we are now leaning into the future by including the Gen-Z sound very deliberately. It is about time that we sync our cords with what the youngsters want. Nostalgia has its place in Season 14 but so does the firepower of a sound never heard before" (*The Express Tribune*, 2021).

The pandering to Gen Z was reflected in the producers' choice of including young rising musicians like Rovalio, Kaifi Khalil, Eva B, Shae Gill, Abdullah Siddiqui, Hassan Raheem, Karakoram, Talha Anjum and Young Stunners, all of whom are under thirty and have been making music on their own, without the assistance of any major recording studios or record labels. While most middle-aged Pakistanis tend to be unfamiliar with their music, the youth (aka population under thirty years of age), which makes up 64 percent of the country (UNDP, 2018) is not just familiar, but is an active listener of the music of the so-called Gen Z sound. A lot of the younger demographic of Coke Studio's audience had gotten bored with the existing format and lineup, and had effectively stopped listening to the songs because the trademark nostalgia that Coke Studio prided itself on had stopped being relevant to the Gen Z. Therefore, when the lineup for Season 14 rolled out, for a change the younger generation was excited. Seeing names like Hassan Raheem and Young Stunners in the lineup was precisely the change that industry observers had been hoping for. And not only was new talent being showcased and highlighted, but they were also being given a chance to create new, original music, instead of sticking to revamped cover songs.

As part of the writing seminar Khadija teaches at the Lahore University of Management Sciences, she makes her class read and dissect Richard David Williams's and Rafay Mahmood's paper on Coke Studio and memory (2019). In the paper, the authors argue that by engaging with the Coke Studio "audio object" through the comments section under its music videos, or in Twitter and WhatsApp conversations, audiences are actually creating a new "prosthetic memory" that creates its own layers of associations and nostalgic callbacks. The paper contested that while many of the Coke Studio covers were heavily criticized, such as 2018's cover of *Ko Ko Korina*, even the criticisms paved their way to creating conversations about the music, comparisons between the original and the cover, or simply allowing the unfamiliar to discover the original source material.

When Khadija discussed the fourteenth season of Coke Studio with her class—all first-year undergrad students with as-of-yet undeclared majors—she was surprised by their mellow responses. It was easy to assume that a seminar hall full of nineteen-year-olds would have been excited about a season where the majority of the featured artists were Gen Z themselves. However, their comments revealed that over the past few seasons, most of them had lost interest in Coke Studio, due to all their songs sounding the same. A few students suggested that their parents were bigger fans of Coke Studio than they themselves were. Interestingly, the songs that most of them were familiar with were "Pasoori," "Kanna Yaari," and "Peechay Hutt," all of which showcased younger talent.

The change in lineup as well as the distancing from the Sufi-rock genres of seasons past is also evident from the music videos themselves. In prior seasons of Coke Studio, the accompanying music videos for the songs were kept deliberately stripped down and bare, emanating an air of a more relaxed, casual atmosphere. This was a stark contrast to the concept of a "traditional" music video, or perhaps more specifically, of the "spectacle of Bollywood and Lollywood," according to Williams and Mahmood (2019). Even if this relaxed and casual atmosphere was also synthetic, it was still in line with the ongoing Coke Studio maxim of "Sound of the Nation" and "One Nation, One Spirit, One Sound," as it claimed a degree of authenticity for itself, due to the aforementioned lack of spectacle which distanced it from Bollywood and Lollywood, and even traditional music videos. It was as if the videos were intended to say "These are real musicians having a professional but fun jam session that isn't at all being filmed and televised and is definitely not being funded by a giant multinational corporation." Super subtle.

However, as discussed earlier, with Season 14 came a different style of music video. Each song was released with a distinct music video that represented a distinct mood and vibe, creating a unique world for that particular song. And while not all of the created worlds were high on the "spectacle," such as for the songs "Thagyan" and "Neray Neray Vas," videos for other songs like "Pasoori," "Mehram," or "Go" definitely were. The careful selection of color schemes, costumes, and props, and the interaction of the singers with the camera rather than with each other not only make the sentiments and atmosphere associated with each song feel markedly different from each other, but also add a degree of theatricality to Coke Studio that hasn't been around for many seasons, if at all. It does, however, act as a callback to the Pakistani music industry in the early 2000s, where artists and bands were releasing music independently alongside big, over-the-top music videos, thereby preserving Coke Studio's commitment to nostalgia.

Postmodern Vibe for a Postmodern Time

What they say about change is true: it really is the only constant. And in an ever-changing world with ever-changing preferences and attention spans, to adapt is the only way to survive. Coke Studio found a gap in the music ecosystem in Pakistan, and very successfully filled that gap for a good century before it began to run the risk of monotony. In this case, change was the very thing it needed for a revival and comeback arc, and so far, it has served it well.

Not only that, but it also helped strengthen the nascent music industry in Pakistan, by allowing newer, younger talent a chance to make it to the mainstream and become accessible to more than just college and university students. It has long upheld its goal of bringing folk artists to the masses, but this time, it extended that same courtesy to indie musicians making music from their bedrooms, while also widening the net of folk artists it gives a platform to. Although it may have seemed like a risk to bet so heavily on the new generation, it was ultimately a risk that paid off, at least for Season 14.

While we were writing this book, the newest season of Coke Studio, Season 15, was released in April. This, of course, meant that in addition to ascertaining what the impact of the strategically and creatively different Season 14 might be, we now also had a moral obligation to actually compare it with Season 15 and see if that impact actually held up, both in terms of audience and creator preferences.

The answer? Both yes and no. What it carries on from its predecessor is the idea of a "song narrative" strengthened both by the song itself, as well as by the accompanying music video. Season 15's seven songs (as of yet), all have elaborate and beautifully filmed videos that feel like they are trying their best, maybe even a little too well, to embody different aspects of Pakistani culture. This is where the newest season deviates. It no longer pretends to uphold the illusion of a jam between musicians, and instead has shifted to elaborate sets, on-site shoots and perhaps even a fair bit of acting. From intricate Sindhi patchwork quilts, to courtyards filled with sunshine yellow marigolds, the sets are detailed, and have evolved to now even including background actors and extras. Jury's still out on whether that's a good thing. Manahil Tahira notes for *The Express Tribune* "That the predilection towards representation eventually becomes a matter of what is seen rather than what is heard begs the question of what is lost when optics do the talking" (2024). By focusing so heavily on video, is Coke Studio ignoring what it does best and what draws in the crowds: the music?

Another thing brought over from Season 14 is the commitment to showcasing new and upcoming talent. This is something the jury doesn't need to deliberate about; everyone wants to see more fledgling musicians being given the platform that has previously been consistently awarded to all the biggest names in music. Names like Babar Mangi, Star Shah, Zeeshan Ali, and Farheen Raza Jaffery have got people talking, and for good reason. Rafay Mahmood in particular raves about the song "2 AM," saying, "Star Shah and Zeeshan Ali are perhaps two of the most talented individuals to have graced Coke Studio in the last couple of years. They are so deeply rooted in tradition that the soul of this one song can outshine the so-called 'gehrayi' and pretentious Sufi motifs of the entire last season in the blink of an eye" (*The Express Tribune,* 2024).

However, the season also faces an unexpected challenge. When Coke Studio finally returned with Season 15 in April, there were many calls to boycott the show due to the Coca-Cola Company being primarily a brand owned by Jewish stakeholders, as an act of solidarity for the ongoing genocide in Palestine. Listenership will be heavily influenced by these factors. Even though Coke is not technically on the Boycott, Divestment, Sanctions (BDS) list, still, passions run high and once the question has been raised, you can't un-raise it. Be that as it may, the episodes seem to be faring decently, with over 10 million views on average on YouTube. As with Season 11's "Hum Dekhengay," Coke Studio must navigate its way around issues like this each season.

Nonetheless, the direction that this current season and the ones following will take will be the real deciding factor on how the new format bodes for the show. But if nothing else, the inclusion of new and upcoming artists, as well as a diverse range of genres is a big step in the right direction. If Coke Studio continues to keep audiences on its toes in terms of where it will go next, and continues to incorporate audience feedback, as it did in Season 14, the show may yet go on.

Bibliography

"A Bop or a Flop? Hasan Raheem and Justin Bibis 'Peechay Hutt' Has Netizens Deeply Divided," *Dawn Images*, 2022. https://images.dawn.com/news/1189566

Abbas, Mohsin. "Elvis of the East," *Dawn*, 2011. https://www.dawn.com/news/672748/elvis-of-the-east

Ahmed, Zeerak. "یہ دنیا," *Hamnawa*, 2022. https://hamnawa.net/p/–43a

Akhtar, Suleman. "Coke Studio Is Making a Mockery Out of Our Culture," *The Express Tribune,* 2012. https://tribune.com.pk/article/11816/coke-studio-is-making-a-mockery-out-of-our-culture

Breton, Ayesha Le. "Coke Studio Is Pakistan's Multicultural Reality," *The Juggernaut*, 2024. https://www.thejuggernaut.com/coke-studio-pakistan-multicultural-music

"Coke Studio Opens Season 14 with Soulful 'Tu Jhoom'," *Daily Times*, 2022. https://dailytimes.com.pk/869130/coke-studioopens-season-14-with-soulful-tu-jhoom/

"Coke Studio Season 10: Yeh dil mange more," *The News*, 2017. https://www.thenews.com.pk/magazine/insteptoday/214788-Coke-Studio-season-10-Yeh-dil-mange-more

"Coke Studio Season 14: Complete List of Artists Dropped!," *The Express Tribune*, December 20, 2021.

"Coke Studio 14 Complete Lineup Revealed," *The Express Tribune*, 2021. https://tribune.com.pk/story/2334664/c

"Coke Studio's latest 'Ye Dunya' Is a Banger with a Message," *The Express Tribune*, 2022. https://tribune.com.pk/story/2343273/coke-studios-latest-ye-dunya-is-a-banger-with-a-message

Haleem, Soomal. "'Kana Yaari' Is Just a Pit Stop on Baloch Singer Kaifi Khalil's Journey," *Dawn Images*, 2022. https://images.dawn.com/news/1190240

Mahmood, Rafay. "Challenges That Face Coke Studio 10," *The Express Tribune*, 2017. https://tribune.com.pk/story/1340491/challenges-face-coke-studio-10

Mahmood, Rafay. "Coke Studio 15: When Zeeshan Ali and Star Shah Arrived at 2AM," *The Express Tribune*, 2024. https://tribune.com.pk/story/2463646/coke-studio-15-when-zeeshan-ali-and-star-shah-arrived-at-2am

"Malang," *YouTube*, uploaded by Coke Studio Pakistan, 2008. https://www.youtube.com/watch?v=OPkfKQpJKXA

Mattoo, Priyanka. "The Pop Song That's Uniting India and Pakistan," *The New Yorker*, 2022. https://www.newyorker.com/culture/culture-desk/the-pop-song-thats-uniting-india-and-pakistan

"Meesha Shafi's Powerful Vocals Open Coke Studio with a Bang," *Dawn Images*, 2022. https://images.dawn.com/news/1186125/meesha-shafis-powerful-vocals-open-cokestudio-2020-with-a-bang

"Netizens Are Hitting Replay on Coke Studio's Upbeat Qawwali 'Thagyan'," *Dawn Images*, 2022. https://images.dawn.com/news/1189708/netizens-are-hitting-replay-on-coke-studiosupbeat-qawwali-thagyan

"Not Everyone Loves Coke Studio's 'Sajan Das Na' by Atif Aslam and Momina Mustehsan," *Dawn Images*, 2022. https://images.dawn.com/news/1189319

Paracha, Nadeem. *Socio-Political History of Pop Music in Pakistan* (Source of publication unknown). 2004. https://sites.google.com/site/nadeemfparacha2/sociopoliticalhistoryofpakistanipop

Paracha, Nadeem Farooq. "Pakistani Pop Music: A Visual History," *Naya Daur,* 2018. https://nayadaur.tv/23-Oct-2018/pakistani-pop-music-a-visual-history

Qureshi, Regula Burckhardt. "His Master's Voice? Exploring Qawwali and 'Gramophone Culture' in South Asia," *Popular Music* 18.1 (1999): 63–98.

Sabeeh, Maheen. "The 'Pasoori' Phenomenon," *The News*, 2022. https://www.thenews.com.pk/print/968464-the-pasoori-phenomenon

@shireenmazari. "Horrendous! Destroyed a Great Classic—Why Oh Why Did Coke Studio Allow Such a Massacre of This Classic Song?" *Twitter*, October 21, 2018, 11:18 AM. https://twitter.com/ShireenMazari1/status/1054029098174038021

SIL International. "Pakistan: Languages," *Ethnologue*. https://www.ethnologue.com/country/PK/

Tahira, Manahil. "Coke Studio 15: 'Aayi Aayi' Is Sindhi on the Surface, Formulaic at its Core," *The Express Tribune*, 2024. https://tribune.com.pk/story/2462648/coke-studio-15-aayiaayi-is-sindhi-on-the-surface-formulaic-at-its-core

Tanweer, Bilal. "Coke Studio," *Critical Muslim* 4 (2012). https://www.criticalmuslim.io/coke-studio/

"'Thagyan' Is a Return to What 'Coke Studio' Used to Be, with a Twist," *The Express Tribune*, 2022. https://tribune.com.pk/story/2347871/thagyan-is-a-return-to-what-coke-studioused-to-be-with-a-twist

Tingen, Paul. "Michael Brook: World Music," *Sound on Sound*, 1995. https://www.soundonsound.com/people/michael-brook-world-music

"Unleashing the Potential of a Young Pakistan," *United Nations Development Programme*, 2018. https://hdr.undp.org/content/unleashing-potential-young-pakistan

Unni, Deepti. "The Challenge of Fusion," *Rolling Stone India*, 2011. https://rollingstoneindia.com/the-challenge-of-fusion/

Williams, Richard Davis and Rafay Mahmood. "A Soundtrack for Reimagining Pakistan? Coke Studio, Memory and the Music Video," *BioScope: South Asian Screen Studies*, 10.2 (2020): 111–28.

"Year in Search 2022," *Google Trends*, Google. https://trends.google.com/trends/yis/2022/GLOBAL/#6547f16f-5b3a-42f3-b43b-32f0be97231b

Index

A-ha 15
Abbas, Fazal 55
Afshaar, Rehman (Maanu) 75
Aftab, Arooj 47, 48, 49
Ahmed, Rabi 51, 71
Ahmed, Riaz 74
Ahmed, Zeerak * 59
Akhtar, Suleman * 2
Alamgir 13
Ali, Asad 72
Ali, Asif 33, 52
Ali, Basharat 74
Ali, Haider 51, 73
Ali, Hashim 56, 57, 58
Ali, Zain 73, 74
Ali, Zain (Action Zain) 31, 51, 71, 73
Ali, Zeeshan 86
Ali, Zohaib 73, 74
Amjad, Joshua 68
Anjum, Talha 59, 60, 61, 77, 78, 81
Arthur, Melvin 73
Aslam, Atif 8, 11, 27, 43, 44, 75, 76
Aslam, Muhammad 74
Ayaz, Fareed 8
Azmat, Ali 7

Bagga, Sahir Ali 10
Baig, Aima 10
Baloch, Quratulain 73, 74
Bayaan 47, 48
Beiber, Justin 63
Bibis, Justin 63, 64
Breton, Ayesha Le * 2
Brohi, Abid 80
Brook, Michael 15
Brothers, Butt 51, 52, 53
Bugti, Wahab 39, 41
Butt, Shamroz 51, 52
Butt, Umair 51, 52

Call 30

Daniel, Haroon 71
Dhool, Adnan 44, 51, 53, 59, 71, 77

Entity/Paradigm (EP) 16, 30
Eva B 39, 41, 81

Faiz, Ahmed Faiz * 9
Fateh Ali Khan, Rahat 7, 8, 43
filmi pop 13

Gill, Shae 55, 56, 57, 81

Hamid, Mohsin * 8
Hamza, Ali 9, 23, 24, 80
Hashmi, Hadiya 51

Hassan, Mekal 17, 27
Hassan, Nazia 14
Hassan, Saad ul 71
Hassan, Shahzad 15
Hassan, Zohaib 14
Hussain, Asfar 47, 48, 49
Hussain, Mehboob 74
Hyatt, Rohail 8, 10, 11, 15, 19, 20, 21, 22, 30

Iqbal, Allama 15

Jaffery, Farheen Raza 86
Jamshed, Junaid 15
Jal 30
Junoon 7, 15

Kaavish 17
Kapadia, Faisal 8, 77, 78
Karakoram 59, 81
Kazi, Zohaib 9, 23, 24, 80
Kazmi, Awais Ali 33
Kermani, Sheema 56
Khaleel, Kaifi 39, 40, 81
Khan, Kamal 57, 58
Khan, Mairah 40
Khan, Nusrat Fateh Ali 8, 11, 15, 16
Khan, Pathanay 14
Khan, Sehar Gul 11
Khan, Ustaad Sharif 14
Khan, Zulfiqar Jabbar (Xulfi) 30, 31, 33, 40, 48, 51, 58, 59, 71, 73, 75, 77
Khattak, Sherry 59, 60, 61
Krewella 25

Lal, Naseebo 33, 34, 35, 37
Lohar, Arif 8
Lollywood 7

Macklemore 69
Madni, Zara 11
Mahmood, Rafay * 80, 82, 83, 86
Mangi, Babar 86
Maqsood, Bilal 8
Marvi, Sanam 11
Mashrequi, Payam 78
Mattoo, Priyanka 57
Mazari, Shireen 43
Mir, Ahad Raza 43, 44
Mohsin, Jugnu 57
Mooroo 80
Muhammad, Gul 75
Mustehsan, Momina 8, 43, 44, 45, 71, 72, 76

Naqab, Rohail 33
Naqvi, Wajiha 11
Naukhez, Annan 60
Nescafe Basement 30, 48
Niaz, Murtaza 52
Noor, Ali 20, 21
Noori 9, 15, 19, 27

Pakistan Television 14
Pandit Ravi Shankar 48
Parveen, Abida 33, 34, 35, 37
Parvez, Zeeshan 35, 60, 77, 78
Paul, Kami 40
Pepsi Battle of the Bands 47
Pervaiz, Fariha 11
Pink Floyd 15
Presley, Elvis 13

Qadri, Ustaad Riaz 25
Qawwal, Abu Mian 8
Qureshi, Regula * 16
Qureshi, Talal 31, 63, 64

Raheem, Hassan 57, 63, 64, 81, 82
Rahman, A. R. 17, 35
Ramay, Yusuf 71
Raza, Asim 73
Rehman, Jamal 32, 41, 79
Reshma 14
Rovalio 81
Roxen 30
Rush 15
Rushdie, Ahmed 13, 43

Sajid and Zeeshan 17
Sethi, Ali 55, 56, 57
Sethi, Najam 57
Shafi, Faris 59, 60, 67, 68, 69
Shafi, Meesha 8, 11, 67, 68, 69
Shah, Bulleh 15
Shah, Star 86
Shan, Veeru 52
Shankar, Anoushka 48
Siddique, Abdullah 30, 31, 34, 35, 40, 44, 48, 56, 58, 75, 76, 77, 81
Singh, Arijit 57
Soch The Band 51
Sohail, Sania 63, 64
SomeWhatSuper 80
Strings 8, 9, 77

Tabedar, Muqadaraan 63, 64
Tahira, Manahil * 86
Tanweer, Bilal * 6
The Express Tribune * 2
Tingen, Paul * 16

Uppal, Shiraz 17

Vital Signs 14, 15

Williams, Richard David * 82, 83

Young Stunners 60, 81, 82
Yunus, Talha 77, 78

Zafar, Ali 68, 69
Zaidi, Jaffer 17
Zeb & Haniya 8
Zohaib, Zain 73, 74